THE ENERGETIC MANAGER

Fred Pryor's System for Unleashing the Power in Yourself and Your Organization

THE ENERGETIC MANAGER

Fred Pryor's System for Unleashing the Power in Yourself and Your Organization

by Fred Pryor

PRENTICE HALL
Englewood Cliffs, New Jersey 07632

Prentice-Hall International, Inc., *London*
Prentice-Hall of Australia, Pty. Ltd., *Sydney*
Prentice-Hall of Canada, Inc., *Toronto*
Prentice-Hall of India Private Ltd., *New Delhi*
Prentice-Hall of Japan, Inc., *Tokyo*
Prentice-Hall of Southeast Asia Pte. Ltd., *Singapore*
Editora Prentice-Hall do Brasil Ltda., *Rio de Janeiro*
Prentice-Hall Hispanoamericana, S.A., *Mexico*

© 1987 *by*

Fred Pryor

10 9 8 7 6 5 4 3 2 1

Library of Congress Cataloging-in-Publication Data

Pryor, Fred.
  The energetic manager.

  Includes index.
  1. Employee motivation. 2. Supervision of
employees. I. Title.
HF5549.5.M63P78 1987   658.3'02   87-25749

ISBN 0-13-277203-5

ISBN 0-13-277179-9 {PBK}

PRENTICE HALL
BUSINESS & PROFESSIONAL DIVISION
A division of Simon & Schuster
Englewood Cliffs, New Jersey 07632

Printed in the United States of America

What This Book Will Do
for You

This book is about human energy—how to get it for yourself, how to share it with your associates, and how to use it to make your organization's dreams become reality.

The most obvious difference between a switched-on, vigorous, ready-to-go organization and one that is lethargic, drowsy, and out-of-steam is the people who work there—the CEO, the top managers, the middle managers, the research and development staff, the accountants and attorneys and economists, the office workers and systems specialists, the sales people in the field, and the people who sweep up after hours. If your organization is energized, you and everybody else who works there knows it. If it isn't, probably nobody will need to worry about it long. In today's competitive marketplace, there is no spot left for laggers.

If, indeed, we define energy as "the ability to do work," then energy is what the workplace is all about. But how do we get energy—and how do we pass it on to others? How do we recognize it when we see it elsewhere—and how do we make it a part of our own office, our own division, or own agency, our own corporate culture?

The symptoms of an energetic organization are as hard to miss as those of a good case of measles. There's new growth, excitement, enthusiasm, dedication, innovation, change—the list goes on. People in an energized environment operate more efficiently, more creatively than others. They seem really to care about the products or services they produce. And regardless of where they perch on the organizational ladder, they have a clear picture of what their organization is all about.

The people who lead energetic organizations aren't bound by charts and pecking orders. They are far more likely to be interested in establishing open communication with their employees, in finding ways to reward them for doing good work, in helping them to advance in their careers.

Energetic—or switched-on—leaders are always looking for meaningful ways to recognize productivity and show appreciation to people who find new solutions to old problems. They are constantly on the lookout for new resources they can offer employees to help them get their jobs done efficiently. Energized managers look for ways to challenge less-motivated employees as well as ultra-bright ones. They make room for creative staff members who hear the beat of a different drummer—and, more often than not, those managers reap rewards for the insight that led them to give such support.

In short, the energized leader who seeks to spread his or her energy throughout the workplace looks for ways to find and reward behavior that is good for the organization. In that way, the manager makes sure such behavior is repeated and magnified.

One simple point I stress is that trust and kindness and caring—the same qualities you find in a loving family—make sense in the workplace. Showing your staff members that you are interested in them as individuals and that you see them as valuable assets to the organization goes a long way toward motivating them.

How you deal with the people and events in your life decides your ultimate success. Keeping your enthusiasm and love for people, your sense of expectation and optimism about your work and your personal life, and sharing those feelings with others; communicating freely and openly about the good things that are happening, as well as the bad; nurturing in yourself the ability to listen; being open to new ideas and flexible enough to change the old; avoiding bitterness and remorse about opportunities lost or relationships ended; and, maybe above all, keeping your sense of the ridiculous and being able to see the humor in situations that cry out for it—all these and more are essential to building energy into your management style and into your organization's structure.

One of the most telling demands life makes on us, both personally and professionally, is change. How we face it—or choose not to—is a good predictor of our success in both our private and work lives. That's why, at the end of every chapter in the book, you'll find a section of "yes, buts…" To use a term coined by a longtime colleague of mine, Harles Cone, I'm "pre-calling" the natural inclination that most of us have to keep things as they are, comfortable and familiar. So before you can come up with an excuse for not changing, I'm thinking of it for you. After all, I've used them all myself at one time or another.

Unfortunately, in the workplace as well as in sports, the players often get so wrapped up in the game that they lose the perspective they need to be able to see what's really happening on the field. In this book, I'd like to stand in as your coach, so to speak, to help you assess the action and point out what might be right or wrong in your own particular game.

As you read these chapters, I hope you'll think of them as conversations between the two of us. When you read a suggestion I've made, say—out loud, if you want to!—"This is how I could make that work." Then, to reinforce the concept, apply it to a situation in your own office or plant or agency. When we've finished our ten two-way conversations, I believe you will have found many practical tips for putting into action the ideas in these chapters.

I'm ready now to begin exploring ways we can infuse you—and your organization—with the kind of energy that will propel you into the 21st century far ahead of your competition. Let's get started on the trip!

Fred Pryor

ACKNOWLEDGMENTS

How can a first-time author ever accurately and completely thank all of the people who have helped him to bring together and focus the ideas, theories, reading, experiences, late-night conversations, elusive quotations and scattered thoughts that make up a book?

This book reflects the people with whom I've worked, lived and talked throughout my career, and it mirrors the audiences to whom I've spoken all over the country since the late '60s. I believe each experience we have in life becomes a part of how we think, how we act, what we believe. And I feel that I've been lucky in the associations I've had through the years. For that reason, it has been a great privilege to try to bring all those experiences together into a collection of thoughts on good business management and leadership.

During the years since 1972 that my company, Fred Pryor Seminars, has been active in the area of public seminar presentation for business, government and non-profit organizations, we have learned from our customers what management is all about. I owe them my thanks for telling me consistently that success in human relationships is the linchpin of good management. My business associates, too, believe what those seminar customers tell us. And a number of them got together with me when the book project first began to take form to talk about the focus it should have. Among those friends and associates who were a part of the early roundtables were Phil Love, Kathryn

Collins, Mike Murray, Del Poling, and others, along with consultants Eugene Raudsepp, Jonathan Schenker, and Michael Turnbull.

Once our format was in place, we called on the writing and editorial skills of Diane Gage and her colleagues, Vicki T. Gibbs and Noonie Benford, whose interest in the book and contributions to it have been invaluable. Susan Tucker, our developmental editor, added good ideas for making the book useful to you, the reader, and helped to bring all its parts together. Certainly, too, we want to thank Tom Power, our Prentice-Hall editor, who first read the book and liked it and ended up patiently guiding us through the publishing process, and Dot Yandle, our special projects consultant, who worked with him to refine the final product.

Within the body of the book, we have made every attempt to give credit to the scores of management theorists and others who have built the enormous reservoir of information we all use today, but that task is an unending one. There are also dozens of writers—Norman Cousins, Steven Corey, William Glasser are just a few—who have influenced my thinking through the years. To them, I owe a heartfelt thank you.

Finally, to my wife Shirley, and to my family, who have supported the book project enthusiastically, as they have all my endeavors, I give my warm appreciation.

F.P.

TABLE OF CONTENTS

What This Book Will Do for You v

Acknowledgments ix

Chapter 1: Conquering Organizational Inertia:
How to Build Excitement into Your Corporate
Structure 1

- Creating a Climate That Cultivates Productivity
  and Teamwork (2)
- Is Tunnel Vision Preventing You from Seeing the Big
  Picture? (4)
- Rallying Employees to Meet Company Goals: Give Them a
  Game Plan (5)
- Motivation—*Not* Automation—Boosts the Bottom Line (7)
- Five "Hot Spots" That Control Organizational Energy (8)
- How to Activate Potential Energy Within Your Company's "Hot
  Spots" (15)
- Tips for Moving into the Future Better Prepared than Your
  Competition (16)
- Flipping the Switch in Your Life and the Lives of Others (18)
- Mobilizing Your Workforce: Develop a Company of Leaders (18)
- How to Stop Passing the Buck and Take Control of
  Your Destiny (20)

Chapter 2: Harnessing the Promise of the Future: Long-Range Planning Is as Good as Goals 23

- Committing to Excellence for the Long Haul (28)
- Going the Extra Mile Brings Gold-Medal Results (29)
- Becoming Your Company's Visionary—What You See Is What You Get (30)
- Meeting the Challenge of Making Your Dreams Come True (31)
- Becoming a Leader Who Deserves to Be Followed (32)
- Staying Flexible Enough to Stretch Your Limits (33)
- One Company Reshuffles the Deck and Finds a Whole New Game (35)
- A Few Believers Can Convert the Masses (38)
- Lessening Your Risk by Managing Change (39)
- New Strategies for Developing a Corporate Mission Statement (40)
- Keeping a Personal Journal to Chart the Progress of Change (41)

Chapter 3: Preserving the Valuable: Unearthing the Full Potential in Ourselves and Others 45

- Attention to the Present Pays Off in the Future (48)
- Four Questions for Assessing Your Company's Strengths and Weaknesses (49)
- How Company Leaders Can Encourage Team Spirit for That Winner's Edge (50)
- Helping Employees Size Up Their Strengths Can Avoid Business Misfits (55)

Chapter 4: Beating the Blues: How to Identify and Eliminate Your Emotional Saboteurs 59

- Unlearning Self-Obstructive Behaviors: Fighting Back When You Are Your Own Worst Enemy (60)
- Sporting a New Attitude: How to Turn Vicious Game Playing into Productive Teamwork (63)

- Let the Momentum of Change Propel You Toward Your Goals (64)
- Meet Employees' Needs and They Will Serve You Well (67)
- Anger Is Fear in Sheep's Clothing (68)
- Worrying: It Gnaws Away at Creativity (69)
- Director, Prima Donna, Understudy—Cast Yourself for Rave Reviews (69)

Chapter 5: Focusing Energy: How to Get More Done with Less Effort 81

- Do Your Actions Reflect Your Values? (84)
- Asking Just One Question Will Help Keep Priorities in Check (89)
- Three Tips for Earning Big Returns on Time Investments (90)
- Organize Today—Because You Won't Have Time to Redo Things Tomorrow (91)
- Scheduling Your Day Around Energy Peaks and Valleys (92)
- Learning to Say "No" to Prevent Interruptions (93)
- Are Telephone Calls Putting a Hold on Your Day? (94)
- The Delegation Factor: It Will Multiply Your Efforts (95)

Chapter 6: Discovering the Power of Positive Management: Tune in to Trust and Receive Cooperation 99

- Management from the Bottom Up: Supporting Staff with Resources and Opportunities (102)
- Invest in People—Don't Use Them (104)
- Cutting the Cord: How to Avoid Employee Dependency (105)
- Are You Making Yourself Look Good at Others' Expense? (106)
- Building Self-Esteem Through a Strong Support Network (107)
- 11 Attributes of a Resourcing Manager (108)
- How Leadership Style Influences Commitment and Intensity (110)
- A Different Kind of PERK That Makes Employees Respond with VIGOR (111)

**Chapter 7: Transmitting Energy: Are Your Communication
Lines Clear Enough to Hear a Pin Drop?** 115

- Are You *Really* Open to Feedback? (116)
- Allowing for Others to Make Mistakes (118)
- Learning to Speak Your Employees' Language Can Open a Whole New Dialogue (119)
- Redistributing Energy Use During Communication "Brownouts" (120)
- Stamping Out Rumors: The Wisdom of Keeping Employees Informed (121)
- It's Not What You Say, but How You Say It: Are Your Tone and Demeanor Speaking Well for You? (122)
- Problem-Solving with a Four-Step Gripebuster (123)
- What You Don't Say *Can* Hurt You: Nonverbals and Extra-Verbals Can Speak Louder than Words (126)
- Opening Up About Cover-Ups: How to Keep the Work Force Informed About Confidential Information (127)
- If You Listen Closely, You'll Discover Three Types of Learners: Which One Are You? (129)

**Chapter 8: Maximizing Energy: Discovering Strength
in Numbers** 133

- Maintaining the Excitement of a Task Force for Everyday Tasks: W.L. Gore & Associates Is a Case-in-Point (134)
- At Stew Leonard's Dairy It's Not *What* They Sell, but *How* They Sell It (136)
- Four Steps to Increase Synergy: It All Starts with *You* (138)
- Composing the Right Employee Mix: Don't Just Look for Carbon Copies (140)
- Using Intuition to Select Staff Members (141)
- Training and Development: The Bottom Line in Human Resources Accounting (142)
- The Hard Lesson of Learning to Play (144)
- Why Rest and Relaxation Are Essential (145)
- Planning a Health and Fitness Program for Your Employees (145)

- How "Play Breaks" Can Improve Your Decision-Making (147)
- You Are What You Have Been Becoming: How You Live Today Maps Your Future (148)

Chapter 9: Tapping New Energy Sources: Mining the Wealth of Creativity and Innovation Within Your Organization 153

- Exploding the Creativity Myth of "Some Have It, Some Don't" (154)
- Innovation—Putting Creativity to Work for You (156)
- Embracing Change Can Open the Door for Growth and Improvement (156)
- Producing Tangible Results by Using Creativity and Innovation (158)
- Allowing Yourself to Be Creative (158)
- Strengthening Your Creative Abilities Through Right Brain Development (159)
- The Folly of Waiting for the Perfect Idea (159)
- Building an Organization That Innovates Can Propel You Toward Your Goals (160)
- Structuring the Innovating Process (162)
- Encouraging "Intracorporate Entrepreneurs" Fuels Growth (163)
- Freeing Employees to Experiment (164)
- Motivating and Rewarding Invites Creative Solutions (166)
- Getting Serious about Play: Learn to Make Allowances for Humor (167)
- Sparking Creativity: Fourteen Steps to Encourage Innovators and Creators (167)

Chapter 10: Converting Potential into Action: Match the Right Amount of Energy with the Desired Result ... 173

- Capitalize on Employee Input to Multiply the Efforts of Your Work Force (174)
- Optimizing Effectiveness: Learn to Redistribute Your Energy and That of Your Employees (176)

- Consistency: The Secret to Professionalism (177)
- Overcoming Obstacles: Refuse to Accept Negative Messages from Yourself or Others (179)
- Fulfill Your Potential by Discovering What Life Is Expecting from You (180)
- How to Escape Your Comfort Zones and Achieve More (181)
- Running in Your Target Zone Will Keep You at the Front of the Pack (182)
- Tacking into the Wind: Using Available Resources to Achieve Your Objectives (184)
- Maintaining the Energy Cycle: Overcoming Fatigue and Renewing Excitement (184)

Index 187

THE ENERGETIC MANAGER

Fred Pryor's System
for Unleashing the Power
in Yourself and Your
Organization

CHAPTER 1

Conquering Organizational Inertia: How to Build Excitement into Your Corporate Structure

WOULDN'T it be great if everyone in your organization had the experience and expertise of a company veteran—plus the enthusiasm and eagerness of a rookie? Think how much more you could get done and how much more fun you'd have doing it.

We've all witnessed employees who start a new job by arriving two hours early with a bounce in their step and a shine on their shoes—only to find months later that the sparkle has faded from their hearts as well as their heels. They shuffle in later each morning and sprint out the door at the sound of the five o'clock whistle. The honeymoon is over.

The same holds true for businesses. Imagine how profitable an organization could be if it had the knowledge and resources developed after years of doing business, coupled with the spirit and excitement the founders had when they first opened the doors? Think what great strides your company could take—in productivity, profits, and employee and customer satisfaction.

Managing a company like this may seem like a pipe dream, but it can become a reality! Your energy and the energy of your employees doesn't have to fade away with the years. It doesn't have to dwindle with the problems that arise when you struggle through growth spurts and "down" times. Instead, you *can* combine experience and know-how with optimism and vigor, in a way that will create new and better ways of thinking.

How can we cheer employees on and help them win job satisfaction that will last for the long haul? By paying attention to a psychological factor that has long been overlooked in management—the *Energy Factor*. There's a specific level of energy in your life and the life of your organization. You can manage that energy—and you can even increase it. This book is intended to tell you how.

Creating a Climate that Cultivates Productivity and Teamwork

There are some similarities between the psychological energy that exists in companies and the physical energy that exists on this planet. Both are precious, limited resources that need to be carefully managed.

Until quite recently, we Americans were oblivious to the need to manage physical energy. For generations, we tended to look at energy as just a means to an end, and we behaved as though we had a plentiful supply of it. Until the first oil embargo of 1973, we jumped into our cars and thought little of the energy required to get where we were going. But then, our whole approach changed: we became aware of energy as a resource in itself. We started to recognize how our own behavior affected that resource. After we stood in lines waiting to pump gas and were threatened by gas rationing, we began to think of ways to conserve the supply—carpooling to work, putting the kids on school buses, consolidating trips to the grocery store, and calling ahead to make sure gas stations in the mountains would be open before we hopped into the car for a Sunday drive. Meanwhile, oil companies poured *their* resources into trying to increase the supply: as the price of gasoline soared, oil companies pushed harder to produce and sell more oil.

Since that first oil crisis, we no longer take oil or any type of energy or natural resource for granted. Huge new industries have developed to manage energy: there are solar-powered electricity generating plants, wind-powered plants, even thermal energy conversion programs that generate power using the temperature differences in ocean water. In fact, our country has witnessed an entire technological revolution since the development of two new devices for using energy—the microchip and the laser beam. We are making better use of physical energy because we are paying attention to it; and as we grow more sophisticated in handling the energy of the physical universe, we open new doors and gain new opportunities.

Meanwhile, what about organizational and managerial energy—the kind this book is about? Do we think pre-1973 in the way we handle that kind of energy? Most of us take it for granted; we don't think about energy as a separate and manageable factor that can be created, enhanced, protected, and preserved. We've certainly experienced those staff "brown-outs" on Friday afternoon when nothing gets done—and we've seen what happens when a new employee comes on board and revitalizes an entire department with new enthusiasm and fresh ideas. But most of us don't realize that in both these situations, the deciding factor is energy. We don't realize that our energy and the energy we emit to our staff can make a difference in how a company and its employees perform.

What do I mean by the Energy Factor mentioned earlier? I like the definition we all learned in high-school science class: energy is simply *the ability to do work*. But I also like the images I get from the word "energy." There's the feeling of electricity in a company's atmosphere when a new product is just about to take off...the steady current of support and ideas that flows from

supervisors to workers and back again in a well-managed department...the power surge a company can get when useful new
productivity-boosting equipment is installed. (Though managers
have to be careful, too, that the organizational circuits are "wired"
heavily enough to carry all that new power—if the workforce isn't
fitted for it, the company may blow a fuse.) There's the laser-like
effect you can get from one sharp employee's mind when he or she
cuts through a bunch of complications to get to the heart of a
problem. And there's even the nuclear explosion that results when
two incompatible managers don't see eye to eye!

Energy is power. It gives an organization the capacity to
produce, and produce *big*, and so must be consciously managed.
Energy can be dangerous if not handled correctly; but if you know
how to handle it, you can do a lot of exciting things—conserve it;
maximize it; focus it; release it...and much more.

The energy we need to manage is a form of psychological
energy, which doesn't come in the light waves we all learned
about in high school; instead it comes from people—in waves of
excitement, enthusiasm, and insight.

To encourage this "people energy", managers must learn to
monitor their organization's overall psychological climate. They
must make conscious changes in the way that people in the
company relate to each other, and they must think about how
the activities of all departments mesh.

Is Tunnel Vision Preventing You from Seeing the Big Picture?

A lot of American companies, and in turn, managers, are
ignoring the prime importance of energy. Many have taken new
steps to build revenue and morale—they're practicing par-
ticipatory management, they're throwing out the old organization charts, and they're beefing up health and fitness programs.
But not all of these managers have recognized that to reach
optimum performance, they must learn to deliberately control
the energy within themselves and their company. Sometimes
managers seem to be hammering hard on just one nail—trying

to deal with just one area or problem, or using a single strategy such as hiring new employees, buying new equipment, or designing a new advertising campaign. If a problem arises in the finance department, the usual response is to hire a new vice-president of finance. And when employees complain about the way they're treated, a human resources specialist is brought on board. But the trouble is, the manager is focusing on just one specific aspect of the operation; while the problem may be one that exists on a wider level.

And here's another typical philosophical stance managers often take: the belief that if each employee gets his or her act together, the aggregate of all their individual efforts will automatically energize the company. This is a mistake: having a company filled with motivated, self-assured employees does not ensure a company's success. Again, the problem may be a larger one: we may need to consider not only what the *people* within the company need, but what the *system* needs as well.

Now, it's time to recognize the role of energy in our organizations and our personal lives. It's time to realize that energy is our life force, and it can be deliberately managed and positively manipulated. In just the last few years, a few special corporate leaders have started to wake up to energy. They've started to see energy as a valuable commodity in itself, not just a byproduct of their hard work; a resource—just like their cash, their industrial plants, and their raw materials. I've visited with some of these managers, and I want to tell you some of the things I've seen.

Rallying Employees to Meet Company Goals: Give Them a Game Plan

Can you imagine the members of a professional football team—players who demand extraordinary salaries—warming up for the Superbowl but not knowing what they are supposed to do once the official blows the whistle? It's ludicrous to think about a professional sports team not knowing the object of the game. Yet it's commonplace for company leaders, who are otherwise procedures-oriented, to give employees few clues about the overall game plan for the company. When most managers interview a potential employee, they just explain the job the individual will be hired to do; they touch lightly, if at all, on the overall goals of the company.

Dick Slember, Ph.D., general manager of the Nuclear Fuels Division of Westinghouse, in Monroeville, Pennsylvania, is an exception to this rule. He doesn't hide his corporate goals from anyone—especially his employees. Immediately inside the door to his office is a wall covered with a mission statement and bar charts that show measures (which he calls "pulse points") that the company uses to track its performance. Attached to each quality measure is a goal. These are the key factors for the success of his business.

One of the division's primary pulse points is to deliver its products on time—100 percent of the time. While that may sound like a rather basic objective, in the nuclear fuel business, on-time delivery is no easy feat. Each multi-million-dollar fuel assembly represents an investment of thousands of engineering manhours, and involves highly sophisticated manufacturing techniques. And because of the industry's tough quality standards, no assembly can leave the plant unless it is defect-free.

The year before Dr. Slember took over his present position, the division fell significantly short of its on-time goal, primarily because demand for the company's products outstripped plant capacity. By focusing management and employee attention on the delivery problem, and the other "business factors" that impacted the division's productivity performance, in less than one year Dr. Slember's division had nearly achieved its goal— only one delivery was shipped late, and by just one day.

You could be a stranger walking into Dr. Slember's office, yet know immediately what goals the division is shooting for. Imagine what his employees know—and how that knowledge increases their determination and drive to meet the organization's objectives. Not only are the goals clear, but progress toward meeting them is measured and made visible to everyone.

Motivation—Not Automation—Boosts the Bottom Line

Another wall in Dr. Slember's office is papered with pictures of employees who are "Star Performers." Those same pictures are featured in a four-color company brochure that recognizes employees for a job well done and encourages them to continue to do their best. The brochure is more than a pat-on-the-back piece however. To him it is an affirmation of the fact that quality work begins with quality people.

While the Westinghouse Nuclear Fuels Divisions are technology-intensive, Dr. Slember recognizes that computers and automation alone cannot solve productivity and quality problems. He is a firm believer in the power of motivation. And he feels that one of the best ways to motivate—and energize—people to do their best is through "empowerment," a word that frequently pops up in his informal talks with his staff. In fact, he is fond of saying, "Automation is important, but motivation is far less costly, and can have an even greater impact on the bottom line."

Empowering the entire work force, to find solutions to division-wide problems is a central tenet of Dr. Slember's management strategy. The need for involvement was emphasized several years ago when one plant with the division encountered an unexpected shortfall in capacity. He helped Westinghouse orchestrate a dramatic step increase in production at that plant. When I asked him how he did it, he replied, "Much of what I'm learning as a manager seems so obvious. We simply talked to the work force and made it clear that increased productivity was needed." In other words, he told his employees the object of the game.

Dr. Slember said that task teams were established that consisted of 40 percent of the work force. With so many people involved, the teams were more likely to clarify goals and find solutions to problems. His hunch was right—witness the quick improvement in plant production. "It's amazing," he said, "when you start treating people like people, they act like people." He wasn't talking about benefits or salary administration. He was talking about working with people to help them understand the goals to be accomplished, and to clarify their particular roles in the accomplishment of those goals.

As Dr. Slember pointed out, it all seems so basic. In any organization, the main ingredient for success is learning how to work with people—yet few schools or job training classes teach us how to do it effectively. Some people, like Dr. Slember, pick up techniques for working with people. But why should we leave such an important ingredient for success to chance, when there are very definite, precise strategies you can use to transform your thinking and actions, and boost your energy and that of your organization?

Five "Hot Spots" That Control Organizational Energy

Is your company's energy level higher or lower than it was last year at this time? Is your energy more focused or less focused? Do employees seem to be running around in circles searching for the company's purpose or are they headed down a straight path toward a defined goal? There's energy—low energy or high energy—in every part of your company, all the way from the CEO's office down through the production department, the employee relations department, and even the mailroom. And how you manage that energy can make a tremendous difference.

Suppose you want to design a system that will control this energy. Where should you start? You should pay close attention to five key areas—areas that are energy hot spots. They are:

1. Human resources
2. Organizational structure
3. External markets
4. Technology
5. Information systems

As you look at each "hot spot" on this list, just consider what has happened within your company in the last six months, the last year, the last five years that has had an impact on your organization's energy within that area. For example, did your organization once hold two-thirds of the market—but has its share dwindled to less than half? Have valued employees left for jobs with your competitors because they didn't feel a sense of commitment or ownership? Are you now importing raw materials you used to produce yourself? Is your new computer system taking up employees' time instead of freeing them?

If you've had problems like these, you may need to work on some of the five energy "hot spots." I'll explain:

Human Resources. Take a minute to think about all that goes on within your company during an average workday. Now, picture your workplace without any employees. (Think what it's like late at night or at 6:00 in the morning!) No matter how advanced your technology and equipment are—no matter how eagerly the market is demanding your product—when there aren't any people at your company, nothing happens.

Your work force is one of your organization's main sources of energy. But we sometimes overlook the importance of this vital resource and how its energy level affects our performance on a daily basis.

First, think how much it costs you to hire and train your employees. Did you know that it can cost up to an employee's annual salary to replace him or her? If an individual makes $35,000, it will cost that much to hire and train a new employee and get him or her up to the speed of the former employee. Moral: The cost of hiring and training employees is so great that most organizations must learn to maximize the efficiency of the human energy they have.

Second, think how crucial it is to keep your employees interested and excited about their jobs and the goals of the organization. Your employees are not the only source of energy within your company, but they are the only conscious managers of it. I remember hiring an employee who said he had always wanted to work for my company. When he started, he was ready to climb mountains for the organization, but two years later, he

HAVE THEM MAKE THEIR OWN COMMITMENTS.

left because the company wasn't what he thought it would be. I hadn't challenged this person—and if employees are not challenged, they will grow stagnant.

We've got to let our employees create new challenges for themselves—for example, by letting them become involved in new projects outside of their main area of responsibility. If we do this, they will regain the spirit they had when they were hired: chances are their thinking will shift from "I'm just an employee, I can't influence the company" to "I have the skills and I *can* influence the company." Employees who are excited about the work their company is doing and who feel that their contributions count, give their organizations a much-needed competitive edge. If we can influence human behavior and attitudes in a positive way, we can increase productivity; the difference between effective and lethargic organizations is *people.*

Organizational Structure. Most people work best in an environment in which they feel flexibility and freedom. To see why this is important, think how fast a worker's energy drains away in the wrong type of structure. Take a bureaucracy: it's the perfect example of a structure with rigidly defined job descriptions and lines of authority. Do you get the feeling that workers are excited and productive in an atmosphere like that? Not usually. The system blocks people's creativity and spontaneity and erodes their confidence. You can even see dullness in the employees' eyes! They become convinced that even if they did have a good story to tell, no one would listen.

In *The Change Masters* (Simon and Schuster, Inc., 1983) Rosabeth Moss Kanter tells the story of a textile company which had always assumed that the high frequency of yarn breakage was merely a cost of doing business. One day, an employee finally suggested a successful idea for modifying the machine to reduce breakage which saved the company a tremendous amount of money. When the managers asked him how he had arrived at the solution, he said he'd been thinking about the solution for 32 years. When asked why he had not said something before, the worker replied, "My supervisor wasn't interested, and I had no one else to tell it to." When organizational structures are rigid and employees feel that management cares little about their contributions, the workers begin to merely put in their time, and feel no sense of ownership in the company.

But if workers know that their opinions are sought after and respected, they become eager to give more of themselves. Marion Laboratories, Inc., an extraordinary company in Kansas City that manufactures and markets pharmaceutical products, has worked hard to shed its hierarchical organizational structure, and has taken steps to maintain employees' morale and team spirit. For example, the typical distinction between bosses and staff members is gone: Marion employees call each other "associates." Similarly, if an associate in one department is working on a project for an associate in another department, the first looks on the second as a client who deserves prompt, careful attention rather than as an annoyance who's adding to his workload.

The same philosophy applies to quarterly meetings. In a traditional company, only the department managers would go; but at Marion, the entire company attends "Marion on the Move" meetings, where they are updated on company performance, profit-sharing and incentive plans. As one of Marion's annual reports puts it, "An employee of a company thinks and performs differently than someone who has ownership, or an equity interest, in the company's operation. One of the reasons for Marion's continued strong performance and high productivity is that its associates participate as part-owners in the company." (That's not an exaggeration. Actually, the profit-owning retirement trust at Marion has allowed several employees to retire as millionaires.)

Should every company copy Marion exactly? Of course not: not every organization may benefit by eliminating titles or retiring employees with a million dollars. But all companies can learn from the spirit that guides the Marion system. If a company's structure is built on respect for the individual and an acknowledgment of his ability to contribute, that company is bound to witness positive change.

External Markets. Your company may be energized internally—but a major change in the market could still cause your company to collapse if you don't pay attention to the energy of the marketplace. Are you listening to your customers? Are you watching the competition and taking advantage of all the energy and information the marketplace offers? If you do, you'll have a better chance to create products the marketplace wants and will support.

Many companies perceive their relationship with their external markets as a war, and think of their customer as being on the opposite side. They huddle in their tents plotting strategies to get their customers' attention, and then come striding out to go on the attack to try to win the customers over. But you don't have to fight against the marketplace. Instead, think of your relationship with your markets as a dance: the customer has the lead, but you both enjoy the rhythm and flow of the relationship. An organization should be like a good dancer—responsive to the customer, its partner.

The car industry has become more responsive to customers in recent years: aut manufacturers used to tell people what to buy; but today they've been listening to input from the market place, adjusting the size and adding creature comforts and safety features. Computer companies, too, have realized they must listen to the consumer. When the computer boom began, companies spent more time competing with each other than supplying the needs of their end users. Today, however, they are learning that customers aren't just interested in new technology; they also want practicality, a nice price tag, and equipment that's user-friendly.

Then there's the story of CB radios—a prime example of how external markets can affect an industry. In the late 1970s, when the speed limit was lowered (because of the *physical* energy crunch), more and more truckers were tempted to speed...and of course they wanted to avoid getting caught by the highway patrol. So the sale of CB radios soared from 1 million to 11 million a year. It happened not because the CB industry had launched a major marketing campaign—but because of an energizing factor that existed in the marketplace itself.

And I bet you can guess which companies were able to capitalize on the CB boom: the companies that had their internal forces geared up *before* the demand. You can operate the same way those smart manufacturers did. Get ready to grow—and let your market point you in the right direction.

Technology. Advances in technology can be a tremendous source of energy within organizations. You've probably seen the robots that a lot of companies are using to speed up assembly lines, and your company may be using computer modems that let you send correspondence in seconds instead of in days. Parallel developments have revolutionized certain areas of medicine: many surgical procedures are performed with a new, more effective tool—the laser beam. But there's a catch. Even though these changes in technology enhance our productive capacity, they also force change on people. And if that change isn't handled appropriately, it can drain the company's energy: when people are asked to do things differently from the norm, discomfort often sets in. What can you do to help your employees adapt to technological change? First of all, be sure you don't force your employees to use the new technique or piece of equipment without explaining its time- and money-saving benefits. Second, let them understand that the new technology is a means to an end, not an end in itself. Often companies install new equipment with a variety of features and don't realize that employees are too busy doing their jobs to learn how to use those features. Or employees rely so heavily on the new technology that they feel they don't have to get personally involved. Instead of thinking about a solution, they ask the computer for one.

Advanced technology should not be seen as a savior. It's a helpful tool—which (if we use it properly) can give us an edge in how effectively and efficiently we get our jobs done. But we must not become so fascinated by it that we ignore all the other energy "hot spots." All the gadgets, buzzers, bells, and whistles in IBM's entire catalog won't save a failing organization.

Information Systems. We're all familiar with the old idea of not letting employees know much about what's going on around them. It's the good old "Mushroom Principle"—keep them in the dark, pile manure on them, and finally can them! But it doesn't work—not any more. Today, many organizations are realizing the power of sharing information with all their employees, rather than guarding it for a selected few.

Progressive managements do not want employees to be kept in the dark about what the company expects of them and what it plans to achieve. And notice that these farsighted managements aren't taking this stand out of sheer benevolence. They have been watching their competitors, and they have seen that the organizations which have made some of the most dramatic strides are the ones that share information with employees. When employees feel included in an organization they often make more magnificent contributions.

James "Jimmy" Treybig, founder-chairman of Tandem Computers, Inc., which makes fault-tolerant computer systems designed to avoid computer failures and loss of data, knows that sharing information with his employees is vital to Tandem's effectiveness. Equally as important is employees sharing information with each other. So he has come up with three main methods of fostering employee communication. One of the more popular ways is the Friday afternoon "beer blast." For the last hour of the workday each Friday, employees gather in the company cafeteria (family members, customers, and suppliers are welcome also) to munch popcorn, drink beer and soda pop, and share information about what's happening at Tandem in an unstructured manner.

As management information systems people would say, "This system is designed to promote the exchange of significant information on a timely basis."

Treybig says creativity comes from sharing ideas: an idea may originally be conceived by an individual, but it has to be nurtured and developed by a group until it becomes significant. That's why, in addition to the Friday afternoon seminar, Tandem offers its employees two other communications benefits: 1) access to an expensive electronic mail network which links employees worldwide and lets them respond back to other employees quickly and 2) their own internal television network which is nationwide. This open communication tradition, evident throughout the Tandem organization, is helping keep employees committed and excited—and helping the organization meet its goals.

How to Activate Potential Energy Within Your Company's "Hot Spots"

So how, as a manager, do you create a high-energy department or organization? By activating the potential energy within these five hot spots. The remaining chapters of this book offer ten methods you can use to evaluate and manage the energy that resides in your five organizational hot spots. These methods include: generating energy, preserving energy, coping with energy robbers, focusing energy, releasing energy, transmitting energy, maximizing energy, tapping new energy sources, and optimizing energy for desired results. Don't panic—these methods won't require you to restructure your company completely. Instead, they give you a new model on which to build your existing organization.

Before we go on, a word of warning. As you start to energize your company, you've got to deal with all the organizational hot spots—you musn't get so bogged down in one area that you ignore the others. You can have the most dynamic people in the world, but if you make a poor-quality product because your technology is outdated, your organization will suffer. And if a change in the marketplace makes one of your prime products obsolete, you'd better have enough energy in your human resources, information systems, and technology to update your product.

Employees, too, can make the same mistake. Don't let them concentrate their energies on any one "hot spot" to the detriment of all the others! Some people are highly structured and organized but can't communicate with others; you could set your watch by the punctual way they meet deadlines, but they alienate their coworkers in the process because they haven't seen the value in learning how to work effectively with other people. At the other extreme, some employees have highly developed people skills—but that's all. They can make anybody feel good at any time, but they don't know how to get things done *on* time. They spend hours talking about developing good personal relationships, establishing rapport, and increasing loyalty, but while their friendships are growing, the company's bottom line shrinks.

My point is: watch out for one-sided people. There's no doubt that different people have different strengths and work-styles; but workers who get their personal energy from just one source and ignore the others are an "occupational hazard"—a hazard to your occupation, that is. Try to find people who pay attention to all facets of their energy; they'll ultimately reap the most personal success, and will contribute the most to the vitality of their organization.

Tips for Moving into the Future Better Prepared than Your Competition

The successful, energetic managers of the '80s are learning to distinguish low energy from high energy in each area and to dial up the energy level where needed. They are realizing that they can make a tremendous difference in any or all of these areas if they *manage energy* as a separate business factor, distinct from money, time, the work force, and other organizational resources. But it's not easy; creating a powerful, constant current of energy to flow through these five areas takes skill, and avoiding uncontrolled energy surges and debilitating brown-outs is a tough managerial challenge. Remember, it takes energy to make energy, and incorporating the Energy Factor into your life and the life of your organization takes work.

I am constantly struggling to make my organization an energetic one—and it *is* a struggle. Even though Pryor Resources is in the business of teaching others how to reach their full potential, we sometimes have difficulty doing it ourselves! Our constant aims are: to make sure the goals of our own organization are clearly stated and understood; to make sure everyone knows what is expected of them; to be certain our employees are adequately recognized for their efforts; and to make sure we are using our technology to its fullest and that we are meeting the needs of our markets. Do we always achieve these aims? No. But we have, at least, identified where the energy in our organization resides, and we're continually working to use it to its best potential.

In the Spring of 1985, the University of Kansas, in Lawrence, Kansas, tested *us* on our own theory. They conducted a communications audit within Pryor Resources to identify things our employees felt frustrated about. Sure enough, the study showed that we had a problem! Our employees were dissatisfied with the feedback we gave them about their work: they didn't get enough. That audit made us face facts: we had a weak spot within our company. What to do? First we organized a task force of employees and gave them a mission: to develop a new system for giving our associates more adequate feedback. The task force recommended that we have companywide meetings at frequent intervals—every six to eight weeks. And instead of our usual once-a-year performance appraisals, they recommended we do two: a formal appraisal at year-end and an informal appraisal at the six-month mark. Raises are based on performance in our organization, and with this system employees could earn a raise at six months if they had improved in areas mentioned in their year-end appraisal.)

That wasn't all. We also set up an incentive program with bonuses for outstanding employees. Our supervisors now have to complete a training program that teaches them how to evaluate associates by standard guidelines, not subjective impressions. And finally, all our associates are now requested to set goals for themselves; when the time for their performance appraisals comes around, they do a written self-evaluation to rate their own progress toward these goals.

For my company, all the effort and struggle have been worth it: we're seeing positive results. Other companies struggling to become energetic organizations say the same thing: they're moving into the future better prepared than their competitors. Even the struggle itself gives them new energy. It gives them new hope and excitement, and keeps them aimed in the right direction.

Flipping the Switch in Your Life and the Lives of Others

Whether you are the company president or the company mail clerk, you can start *now* to unlock the energy within yourself and your organization. How? You have to realize that you are the boss of your own life, and you have to accept the responsibility attached to that role. You have to realize that no matter who you are, you are already a leader—or have the potential to be a leader.

Think of it this way. Before the charcoal in your barbecue can become useful energy, someone has to put a lighted match to it. It's the same way with your energy: before it can start to flow, someone must "turn the switch." Leaders are those individuals who know how to "turn the switch" within their own lives, or in the life of an organization, and make things happen. Turning the switch means unlocking the potential that's there: harnessing human resources and transforming energy into results. But notice this: *The ultimate responsibility of a leader is to facilitate other people's development as well as his own.* And to do that, you have to develop a lifestyle, not just a leadership style. The principles you use to make your organization effective are the same ones you use to enhance your personal life: chances are if you are having problems in your personal life, those problems will sooner or later get you in trouble at work too. How can you feel energized at work if you spent half the night fighting with your spouse and half the morning at work thinking about how to make amends? The fact is, if you want to be a leader you have to devote yourself to feeding and cultivating *all* areas of your life—not just your work. If you do, though, you'll begin seeing rewards in all spheres.

Mobilizing Your Workforce: Develop a Company of Leaders

Consider the typical business manager who has a good marriage and a couple of nice kids, but for some reason feels bored with his personal life. Imagine what could happen if he or she could increase the energy level in his family by just 10 percent. Just a few small adjustments—like maybe an-out-of-town weekend for just Mom and Dad, or getting involved in the kids' school projects—could make a tremendous difference! The same approach applies on the job. Let's say you've put together a task force to solve a certain problem. The people you've chosen are all capable, and you're sure they'll do a good job. But what would happen if you could mobilize these people to dedicate 20 percent more energy to that task force?

At W.L. Gore & Associates, Inc., there is a group of employees who are actually giving that extra 20 percent. Gore & Associates is a chemical fabrication company in Newark, Delaware, known for the development of Gore-Tex—a fabric used in athletic clothes and equipment. The fabric lets the perspiration out without letting the elements in. Gore employees—who are known as associates, like those at Marion Laboratories—work within a loose organizational framework called a "lattice structure": they are free to move within the organization and do whatever needs to be done, or whatever intrigues them most. One machine operator, for example, became bored with his job, so he began working on the development of a whole new product. It turned out that this new challenge was just the impetus he needed to find new energy, and soon he became manager for the product! According to the late Wilbert Gore, founder of the company, employees there are given authority commensurate with the responsibility that they are willing to assume.

How does it work? Gore once explained to me that the company is based on direct transactions between people. The key is people's own self-commitment: they have to develop their own natural leadership because the company doesn't assign authority to anyone! "We don't manage people here, they manage themselves," Gore said. "If a person needs to be told what to do and how to do it, he will have trouble adjusting at our company. There are two kinds of associates, those who are 'time-committed' and those who are 'task-committed,' and you're rewarded if you are the latter." Gore explained that the company tries to encourage employees to build their leadership skills; it tries to make workers want to contribute to the enterprise, and want to assume responsibility too.

How to Stop Passing the Buck and Take Control of Your Destiny

People who live their lives as leaders don't blame others when things go wrong. Instead, they take responsibility for making things happen. You know how after an unproductive business meeting people try to find someone to blame? They'll point their finger at someone who was disruptive or lethargic and blame the bad meeting on him. But a person who is a leader, not just a manager, won't waste time doing this. Instead he'll assert himself and start persuading other people to do something productive—now. A manager simply works with what he's given; a leader, on the other hand, exerts some extra energy and takes the initiative to *make* things change when necessary.

Jacob Bronowski's book, *The Ascent of Man*, (Boston, Little, Brown, 1974), really fascinates me, because he claims the difference between man and other animals is that man has the ability to invent, create, and take charge of his own destiny. I believe this applies to our everyday lives! When a person realizes he is in charge, he begins to deliberately *take* charge and make things happen. When he starts to turn potential energy into kinetic energy, that's when he starts to ascend.

Try applying the same principle to your own development and the development of your organization. You know what will happen? You'll begin to look at problems, issues, and challenges in a new light. Instead of asking how you can get the most out of employees, for example, you'll ask what you can do to maximize their energy level. Instead of wondering why changes aren't occurring, you'll realize that you can become the change agent to make things happen. You'll find that factoring energy into your life this way is like making an investment in yourself and your career. It takes energy to make energy: you'll have to expend energy to become energetic. But it'll take less energy than you'll spend trying to catch up with others if you don't make the effort now.

Try it today: you'll begin doing many of the things you've always wanted to do, and you'll do them better than you ever imagined.

"Yes, but..."

All this talk about energy sounds good on the surface, but do you think you'll have nothing but problems if you try to implement the principles? Are you wondering:

—"Yes, but how does increasing energy affect the bottom line?"

Remember you'll get better results from people who have put their heart, their mind, their body, and their soul into what they're doing. If people do their jobs halfheartedly, your organization will probably suffer financially as well as emotionally. When people feel good about their jobs and feel committed to the organization, they invest more of their energies in their jobs. The bottom line increases proportionately.

Or, maybe you're thinking:

—"Yes, but we don't have time to coddle our employees."

If that's the case, remember that it takes less time to deal with employees humanistically than it does to manipulate them. Don't think of energizing employees as coddling them, think of it as an approach similar to "Tough Love," a support group for parents of problem teenagers, which teaches parents to handle their offspring with loving firmness. In an energetic organization there's accountability built into the system as well as freedom. Put them both in, with the belief that your employees *want* to contribute to your organization's success.

CHAPTER 2

Harnessing
the Promise of the Future:
Long-Range Planning
Is as Good as Goals

Many people over age 35 remember when their bodies were trimmer and their muscles were tighter. It seems that one of the occupational hazards of approaching middle age is that health and fitness take a back seat to more pressing responsibilities at work and home. Instead of making an effort to stay in shape, people often try to slide by, hoping that the physical conditioning they did in their younger years will carry them. By the time they realize that they can no longer button the old letterman sweater and that "working out" has grown to mean climbing the stairs to bed, they usually have to expend enormous amounts of time and energy to get back in shape.

Just as we put off planning for the future in our personal lives, we also try to live off past investments in our professional lives. But the trouble is, trying to run off of old energy can eventually catch up with the company. Here's one example: eight years ago the management staff of a large manufacturing company bought some new, beautifully tuned machinery. The equipment ran well, so the company ignored the service contracts. Then, six years later, the company was faced with a choice: it could spend one-half million dollars on preventive maintenance for the equipment or it could use the same sum of money for executive bonuses.

Cruises to the Caribbean captured the vote! But while the company brass basked in the sunshine, their equipment was deteriorating and growing tarnished from neglect. Two years later, when a new management group took over the company, it inherited dilapidated equipment that required costly repairs. As you'd expect, the majority of those problems could have been avoided if the former management had seriously considered the company's future.

It's easy to fall into similar traps dealing with the people who work for us. We often go to great lengths to train new employees, but as the years go by we grow lackadaisical; we fail to invest in our employees' training and development. Their skills become antiquated and their minds become drained.

In our eagerness to satisfy immediate needs, we sometimes do just what we need to do to get by, and we don't take time to maintain our bodies and minds or the equipment and people in our companies. Instead of being positioned to leap into the future, we go on for months basically unprepared, while the future creeps up on us. If we took time to plan in the first place, we'd gain more energy to face what tomorrow holds, and we'd accomplish more.

And here's another problem: while we may *know* the benefits of planning for tomorrow, many of us still fail to *do* it. We make excuses like, "I'm too busy," or "Even if I took time to plan, I wouldn't do it effectively." Or we get bogged down in our organization's complex long-range planning forms. We put off planning until the last minute, and then crank out something in a desperate rush to meet our deadline.

How can we make the planning process easier? We could make it *seem* less formidable if we realized that most of us are naturally good planners. We have the skill, but we just don't recognize it—because so much of our planning is done on an informal basis. Take a moment to think of all the sophisticated planning you do when you drive home from work. First, you envision the place you're going. You determine which route will be most expedient, considering the time of day. And even after you're on the road, you may do more planning: if you spot a traffic jam you quickly alter your plan by getting off the freeway and catching an uncongested side road that will get you home more quickly. See how effective you are at planning every day?

The next time you sit down with your long-range planning forms, remember the skills you use when you plan your drive home or run errands. Before you begin making plans for your department or division, be certain that you understand the direction in which your company is moving. If the company's strategic plan is unclear to you, ask for additional information— or talk to the people who are responsible for the organization's long-range plan. If it's the planning forms that are tripping you up, your company may be flexible enough to allow you to draw up forms that are simpler, less time-consuming, and maybe even more interesting. Once you determine what you can do to make the planning process more inviting, you'll realize that you *have* been a capable planner all along.

In fact, you can do more than just plan for one area, like sales or production. You have the ability to expand your entire vision for the future beyond what you could ever imagine. To test this ability, try this simple exercise: Stand up. Plant your feet shoulder-distance apart and extend your arms straight out to the side. Turn as far as you can to the right, look over your right index finger and mentally mark that spot on the wall. Return to center. Now, put your hands on your waist. This time, turn as far to the right as you can and let your eyes go as far as they will possibly go. Return to center. Finally, extend your arms again and turn as far as you can to the right and determine how far your eyes can see. Return to center.

My guess is that once you saw where you had marked the spot on the wall the first time, you were able to expand your vision on the second attempt by at least 20 to 40 percent. And what's exciting is that if we are willing to give ourselves the opportunity to expand our vision for ourselves and our organizations, we can easily increase our "visioning" capacity by 20 to 40 percent.

I was in high school when I first decided that I wanted to expand the vision I had for my life. It all started when my dad moved the family from Kansas City, Missouri, to a farm in Pleasant Hill, Missouri. (To give you an idea of how I felt about the move, you should know that I had planned to play football for the Westport Tigers and ended up playing for the Pleasant Hill Roosters!) Well, I spent three years on a farm, milking cows and shoveling stuff. Then someone told me that if I got a college education, I might not have to milk cows and shovel stuff. That's when I got my vision. In fact, you might say that when it was time for college, I didn't *go* to get an education, I *escaped* from the farm. In fact I got three academic degrees, in the hope that I was never going to shovel stuff again. (Some of my friends tell me that what I do today is not far off from that activity, but I try not to believe that!)

About age 35, I felt stymied in my career, and once again wanted something new to strive for. It seemed that many of the people I had gone to school with were doing so much better than I was, but I had no idea how to get to that level of achievement. For a while, I kept waiting for Santa Claus—for someone to bring me good fortune or for luck to find me. But then I realized that, even though comparing myself to other people gave me the incentive I needed to improve, it really didn't serve any other useful purpose. Rather than thinking about other people, I needed to discover and release my *own* potential. I began to understand that few people are ever truly lucky. Most of the people we think have had great luck have simply tried harder or longer than us. As the saying goes, luck is where preparation meets opportunity.

I decided to get off my "buts"—to stop making such statements as "I could do that, but . . ." or "I would have been as successful, but . . ." Instead of making excuses for not trying or putting myself down for not being as successful as other people (which only drained my energy), I set some challenging—but attainable—goals. I focused on achieving new heights rather than dwelling on how far I had to go. The more positive reinforcement I gave myself, the more things began to change. I began to see that I was the product of my most dominant thought. Have you ever considered that? Our brains contain 13 to 15 billion cells and are enormously powerful tools. But regardless of all that horsepower, whatever we allow to occupy our minds controls us. What our thoughts tell us makes all the difference in the world. I remember hearing Vice Admiral James Stockdale say, after surviving 7 ½ years of incarceration and torture during the Viet Nam conflict, "It's not what others do to you, but what you do to yourself."

With this new attitude, I discovered that the kind of future I wanted wouldn't be created overnight; it involved a number of steps. I realized that as soon as I met one goal, I could stand on the shoulders of that effort and reach the next one. Then, if I kept actively involved in my business, if I read, prepared, and talked with successful people, I could reach another goal. I'd stand on the shoulders of that goal and eventually make good progress toward where I eventually wanted to be.

Now it's clear to me that what I was doing each time I set a goal, reached it, and moved on was *visioning for the future.* I was seeing beyond the present, much as a Karate student is taught to break a brick with his bare hand by seeing beyond it. Visioning can also be a key to planning for your organization. It's a process that allows you to think ahead to where you want to be and what you want to be doing, and to create workable plans to lead you there. It's planning in a way that is somewhat different from the traditional long-range goals because it allows you to remain flexible to incorporate change.

My first vision for my speaking career, for example, was to give talks to universities and business groups. At that time, national seminar companies were unheard of. But slowly I began to broaden my vision and eventually I imagined—and created—the first one-day seminar company.

Committing to Excellence for the Long Haul

It's important to remember that we must constantly fine-tune our vision. And we mustn't put ourselves down for not having thought of something originally that could have made a difference in setting goals. Planning is like driving. When we drive we focus on two distances: down the road—to anticipate possible occurrences—and directly in front of us for immediate hazards. We adjust our driving accordingly. Likewise, we have to be willing to adjust our planning to accommodate hazards and obstacles.

Visioning is not a single event, it's an ongoing process. But just as it's easy to have 20/20 hindsight, it's also easy to fall into the trap of arriving at a particular goal, reveling in the glory and forgetting to think about new goals. Many individuals and businesses become has-beens because they forget that they must never stop visioning.

Ensuring ourselves of a successful tomorrow means we have to live with vigor and commitment today. Albert Schweitzer, the German philosopher and Nobel Peace Prize winner, was said to have summarized his zeal for accomplishment by saying simply, "I have a lot of things to do." Also known for his work as a physician, musician, clergyman, and missionary, Schweitzer lived his life with purpose to the day he died at age 95.

That sort of spirit reminds me of my father's dedication to life. My dad loved to play the vibraphone, and he used to tell me, "Fred, I'm 73 years old, and I'm still practicing, but I love it. And I hope I'm practicing the day I die, because I want to go out in a flame of glory." And do you know what? My father did play the vibraphone the day he died. I guess you could say that he always tested himself. He never quit practicing because he wanted to be better tomorrow than he was today.

Going the Extra Mile Brings Gold-Medal Results

Desire is an essential component of success. In fact, there's a story about Socrates that hammers this point home. A young man once asked Socrates to teach him all he knew. Socrates took the student to a river and pushed him under the water. When the young man thrashed his way to the surface for air he asked Socrates what he was trying to do. Socrates told the man that when he wanted to learn as badly as he wanted to breathe, he would learn. Socrates knew that people who get extraordinary results aren't more knowledgeable and don't necessarily work harder than anyone else, but they work with intensity and passion.

On a scale of one to one hundred, how much effort are you willing to expend to reach your goals? According to Italian economist Vilfredo Pareto (1848-1923), most people do about 80 percent of what it takes to be effective? It's often not until you realize that you desperately want something, that you'll give the extra 20 percent it takes to reach your goal. It's too bad we can't live every day with 100 percent commitment—the kind that Albert Schweitzer and my father had. Instead, we live our lives in a way that recalls the Greek mythological character Sisyphus, who toiled for hours to push a huge boulder up a hill. Just when he reached the top, the gods flipped the stone down the hill and Sisyphus had to start over again at the bottom. Do you almost reach the top of your mountain only to find that someone or something has blocked your chosen path and you have to start over? Or could it be that *you* are sometimes responsible for not meeting your ultimate goal?

One reason we don't attain our goals is that we often focus on how far away we are from feeling satisfaction rather than how far we've come. When we try to lose weight, for example, we give ourselves two weeks to reach our ideal weight. If, after two weeks of dieting, we step on the scale and realize that we still have eight of the ten pounds to lose, we become discouraged and drown our sorrows by diving into a piece of chocolate cake. But instead of that type of all-or-nothing approach, what if we set some incremental benchmarks in between our present weight and our goal weight and celebrated every time we met those goals? I bet before we knew it, we'd be at our desired weight.

Another way to go the extra 20 percent is to employ "The Law of the Slight Edge." If most people do 80 percent of what it takes to be successful, think how much further ahead you'd be if you expended just a little more effort each day. After a few weeks, months, and years, the cumulative effort would add up to a significant difference. An example is that even if you stopped watching one hour of television a day, you'd gain 44 eight-hour working days a year! The Law of the Slight Edge can be effective in your marriage as well. What would happen if you invested just a little more energy in your home life? If your spouse is going grocery shopping, go along with him or her and use that time to talk and enjoy each other's company. As those little extra efforts accumulate over 10, 20, and even 50 years, you'll reap enormous returns in your relationship. When you hear someone complain that few people have good personal or business relationships and experiences, remember that many people don't have what they want because they are not investing enough energy—not because the opportunities are not available to them.

Becoming Your Company's Visionary—What You See Is What You Get

Psychiatrist and Doctor of Social Relations Elliot Jacques is so convinced of the value of investing in the future that he believes people should be paid on the basis of how far into the future they think—their "time horizons." He says that hourly workers typically have an hour or day's time horizon. That is, they are only concerned with what they will do in the next hour or the next day. Supervisors, he says, sometimes have a week or month's time horizon, whereas managers may have a year's or five-years' vision. And it's the company's leaders who perhaps have a horizon of 25 years and, in turn, should be paid accordingly.

I bet Jacques is right about the benefit of compensating employees for their time horizons. People need to be convinced that there is some reward for being visionary. They may get personal satisfaction, they may get a promotion, or they may imagine new possibilities that might lead to creative developments. They need to realize that if they live a hand-to-mouth existence—thinking only about the present—they won't see how what they do today will influence their lives or their company's life next week, next month, or during the next ten years.

To think in terms of time horizons, project yourself five and ten years into the future and try to make decisions based on where you want to be at that time. To learn to do this, first try to use a technique called "retrospecting." This involves looking back over the past to project the future. Here's how it works: on a blank piece of paper, list three positive things that have happened to you during the last five years as a result of your strengths. Based on what has worked in the past, try thinking to a future time horizon and develop an image of the future you desire.

When I'm running in the morning, I often use that time to "visit" my time horizons and do some long-range planning. I picture myself at age 75 and think how nice it would be to still be running at that age instead of vegetating. Imagining myself 25 years from now gives me the impetus to live my life with more vigor today. I realize that I may never live to see my 75th birthday if I don't exercise, eat right, and manage my stress now. So you can see that long-range planning doesn't mean I don't think about how I will live my life today—in fact, it helps dictate it.

Meeting the Challenge of Making Your Dreams Come True

We can use the same techniques in our organizations. One way to unfreeze a company is to look back and determine where the organization is today compared to five years ago. Seeing where you are and where you want to be creates a challenge. Another way to step up momentum is to say, "Let's see if during the next six months we can . . ." Or even better, encourage management to ask employees what challenges they'd like to set.

You might consider bringing in employees from other companies who have some of the spark your organization lacks. That's much like the farmer who showed an ostrich egg to his hens and said, "I just wanted you to know what others are doing." Or you might want to give employees experiences in other environments, such as training seminars or visits to other companies, so that they can broaden their perspectives and gain new insights.

Another way to interest employees in the company's vision is to ask them to write out a statement of goals for the organization. You'll be interested in and surprised by the different perspectives and preconceptions employees have. This exercise will help you identify your employees' time horizons and may show you why some of your people have a difficult time staying on the course the company has charted.

Becoming a Leader Who Deserves to Be Followed

One of the characteristics of people who assume leadership (even if they don't have the official title) is expansive vision. They see how what they do today affects tomorrow. By contrast, people who have a nearsighted, per-task mentality put little thought into the future—either in their personal or business lives.

I like the way the Eskimos handle leadership. They don't elect leaders; they simply follow the individual who deserves to be followed. Today, you may have some of the best visions in your company and people may like what you're saying. Tomorrow, someone else may have a better vision and you may be eager to follow his picture for the future. But if you are a true leader, you will know that if you keep your options open and continue to be aware of what is happening around you, others will follow you again. Never turn the controls of your life over to someone else. If you do that, you may be overwhelmed by someone else's confidence and ability; and the more they say and do, the less confidence you'll have. Remember that you have the capacity to think creatively and be visionary. Just think about Art Frye-at 3M *who within the framework of his company* used his vision to create and develop the adhesive note into a million-dollar business. But don't use the excuse that people like Art Frye-are smarter than you or have special talents. Instead, use their vision as an example and a source of motivation.

It also helps to know that most successful people have doubts about their abilities along the way. In fact, some still think that their success is a fluke—they suffer from what's known as the Impostor Phenomenon, a term coined by Pauline Rose Clance Ph.D., author of *The Impostor Phenomenon: Overcoming the Fear That Haunts Your Success* (Peachtree Publishers, Ltd., 1985). Despite their high levels of achievement and professional recognition, people with this phenomenon attribute their success to luck, good looks, or timing—anything other than skill and intelligence. Movie actress Sissy Spacek says she's a victim of the Impostor Phenomenon but that she will milk the opportunities for all their worth until she's found out. Try to overcome your doubts by establishing in the forefront of your mind a clear picture of what you've accomplished, what you've done and what it will take to reach your next milestone. Most importantly, accept yourself unconditionally. Don't fall into the trap of saying that you will like yourself if you achieve a certain goal. Instead, appreciate yourself today as you set new goals for tomorrow.

Staying Flexible Enough to Stretch Your Limits

One of the biggest obstacles preventing us from reaching our goals is the fear of the changes we know must take place if we are to grow. It's interesting that most children love the opportunity to change. They see change as the possibility for something new and exciting to occur. Most adults, however, think of change as something scary and threatening because our mind instantly plays back all the failures we've experienced in the past when we tried to do something different.

The book *Take Effective Control of Your Life*, by William Glasser (Harper & Row, 1984), presents a vivid image of the idea of how the photo albums we carry in our minds affect us. My guess is that you probably have pictures in your mind about your job, your marriage and family, and your friends. While good pictures are not harmful, bad pictures can cause our thinking to blur.

Many years ago my youngest daughter, Becky, developed anorexia nervosa and shrank from about 100 pounds to 66 pounds. (Incidentally, if you saw her now you'd never suspect she'd been sick for a day.) During that time in her life, though, Becky's picture in her mind of what an attractive girl looked like was skinny—as skinny as possible. In fact, I read the results of some research in which they took pictures of dozens of anorectics, duplicated the shots, and cut off the heads. Then they pasted them on top of body types ranging from rather portly to the skinniest person they could find. They asked the anorectics which person they would prefer to look like. You know what they said? None of them; they were *all* too fat.

Like the anorectics, some of us have some distorted pictures inside our heads. We need to realize that we control what we paste into our mental photo albums. When we think about making a change, we should realistically ask ourselves if it could be time to replace an old paradigm or behavior with a brand new picture. Thomas S. Kuhn, author of *Structure of Scientific Revolutions* (University of Chicago Press, 1970), says that there is nothing more threatening to man than the thought that the dominant paradigm—the pattern or set of rules by which a group of people lives—is failing. But change is essential. In fact, Kuhn writes that Arnold Toynbee, who has written many books on the civilizations of man, observed that all 26 of the civilizations that have existed in history perished for the same reason: They guarded the paradigm that once made them famous far longer than they should have. Eventually the civilizations cracked from their rigidity and their refusal to yield to new concepts. Do you think the same could hold true for people and companies? I certainly do.

One Company Reshuffles the Deck and Finds a Whole New Game

One industry which determined it could no longer operate on an old paradigm and has made substantial changes is the banking industry. Deregulation, fluctuating interest rates, and increased competition have caused financial institutions to change the way they do business.

"For years, banks were driven by what the government wanted them to do, rather than what the customer wanted them to do," explains Robert Adelizzi, president of Home Federal Savings and Loan, a financial services and real estate lending company that operates more than 160 retail banking offices in California and makes commercial business and real estate loans throughout the country. "We had to take a company that had historically been a mutual institution where there was no stock ownership, and convert that to a stock-owned institution. For 50 years, we had two publics to satisfy: the employees (and officers) of the company and the customers. Suddenly a third public was added—the stockholders, who own a large portion of this company. The changes in ownership and market structure were revolutionary changes for an organization to deal with in a relatively short time frame."

To make those changes, Home Federal took a serious look at its strengths and weaknesses. "Our organization was very good at making employees feel that they were part of a family," says Adelizzi. "But it was really poor at demanding performance out of people."

To many employees, being part of a family meant that the rest of the family members would cover for them if they weren't as good as they should be. Home Federal had a number of senior managers who had been in their jobs for years and were very good at telling the other guy how to do his job, but not as good at doing their own. "That's what happens when people get stuck into boxes within an organizational structure," explains Adelizzi.

According to him, the company's first challenge was to break down that very structured view of the organization. Top management was faced with two options—get rid of those paternalistic managers or move them into new jobs and see how well they could adjust. They chose the latter.

"We took the retail banking guy, who for years had been telling marketing how to do its job, and made him responsible for marketing," says Adelizzi. "We made drastic changes like that throughout the management layer, but didn't significantly touch the other layers of the organization. You couldn't make this type of change in a technical position, but in the more generally oriented management positions, it worked."

Adelizzi believes the management changes helped Home Federal to redefine teamwork. "People had always talked about teamwork, but most of them thought it meant, 'Sure, I'll support that manager if I have to.' Now they had to support him because they had left the world they knew so well and truly were walking in the other guy's moccasins."

Adelizzi says that many survived the change and became better managers as a consequence of it. "We learned who were the survivors and who could make the necessary adjustments," he says. Subsequently, they have taken the strongest managers and determined how to best use their strengths. In areas where they weren't satisfied, they brought in new managers, and continued the process of evolving the management structure and the organization to meet the changing environment.

"An inflexible organizational chart can be an anchor that drags down the organization rather than a rudder that gives the company direction and helps chart a smoother course," comments Adelizzi.

One essential element that evolved from Home Federal's changing culture was a new emphasis on the strategic plan.

"Previously, we didn't need a strategic plan because in a highly regulated business the government dictates the plan," explains Adelizzi. "We tended to attract managers who liked to be told what to do. Now, we wanted to develop managers who could think as individuals and who were willing to express their concerns for the direction of the organization. So, we made sure that our managers understood that part of their job was to plan how their department fit into the overall corporate scheme.

"For years some managers had grumbled about certain regulations; finally we were giving them an outlet for expressing their concerns so that the organization could take a fresh look at managers' ideas and help give them what they needed to make those ideas work."

Another major change that grew out of deregulation was the realization that Home Federal needed to become a market-driven organization. "We had to understand what the market wanted and target our products to the market niches that we were best able to serve. And we had to develop a marketing orientation that would differentiate us and our products from other savings and loans. We tried to change our self-image from 'order takers' to 'salespeople' who provided the best service possible. We began calling our customers 'clients' and our branch managers became known as 'sales managers.' We've developed incentive programs based on how effective sales managers are in delivering quality customer service to our clients."

A large part of the company has responded very well to the change, Adelizzi reports, but there are certain managers who just can't adjust to the idea that their job isn't to sit behind a desk and answer questions. Their role is to actively generate new business and take care of the present customers. Home Federal employees who are successful in the new environment are the ones who realize that every program has to be designed to provide clients with a better product or service and to produce a better profit opportunity for the company.

Adelizzi is encouraged by how well so many of Home Federal employees adapted to the changing environment and embraced the art of selling. "Many said a savings and loan company couldn't become an effective sales organization, but we're proving the detractors wrong. Every effective professional needs to be able to sell himself and his products and services— whether he's a lawyer making a case to a jury, a legislator sponsoring new legislation, or a company president addressing the board. Reduced to the bottom line, selling is what business is all about. Unless you have the power to convince others of the soundness of your conviction, you'll never achieve your goal."

A Few Believers Can Convert the Masses

I agree with Adelizzi. We must believe in the changes we are planning to make if we want others to buy into those changes and help us reach our goals. But don't think that you must have the endorsement of the majority of the people within an organization before change can be implemented. In his book *Diffusion of Innovations* (Free Press, 1982), Everett M. Rogers says that when 5 percent of society accepts a new idea, it becomes embedded in the population. When 20 percent agrees, it's unstoppable.

To convince others that change is necessary, realize that even a small group of "believers" can make a difference. In an organization of 100 people, you only have to convince another 14 people before your ideas will begin to take hold. The momentum you create as others start to agree with the changes you suggest will give added push to the cause. Regardless of what you do, a certain number of people will resist. But you'll have greater hope and more motivation if you realize that you only need 20 percent of the people to support you—not 100 percent.

Larry Wheeler, vice president of communications for Marion Laboratories, a Kansas City-based manufacturer and marketer of prescription and over-the-counter pharmaceutical products, believes that people endorse change more readily when they see that the change is for the better. "When our associates [Marion's term for employees] know that a change will allow us to service our clients more effectively, or respond to physicians more quickly or patients more directly, the change to be implemented is less traumatic."

Lessening Your Risk by Managing Change

Wheeler says that an outside consultant recently asked Marion President Fred W. Lyons, Jr. what business Marion was in. "Mr. Lyons described our company in the way he always does, but the consultant respectfully submitted that that isn't the business Marion is in at all. The consultant said that over the next 10 years, the business we will be in is the business of managing change within our company, our industry, and our nation. He said that if we don't have our knees bent—if we aren't flexible—then we won't be in business for very long. As we thought about that we realized that change is indeed the business we are in. As the industry becomes more competitive, as foreign companies become more active in our market, as generic drugs impact the industry, we have to be responsive to those changes and manage them well, or frankly, they will leave us behind."

Wheeler believes that companies can control the changes facing them by determining how much risk they are willing to accept and how they will manage it. "We are involved with the development and marketing of pharmaceutical products," says Wheeler. "There is an enormous number of risks—one out of every 100 new drugs makes it to the market, the average cost to get a new product to market is $80 to $100 million, and it takes seven to ten years. Many companies that we compete with in this industry do what we call synthesis of molecules, the development of an entirely new compound that will have an effect on the bodily system—whether it be an anti-ulcer compound or a heart medication.

"Our philosophy," Wheeler continues, "is that we don't have the critical mass to support that kind of activity. We can reduce the amount of risk associated with research and development by going to other parts of the world and licensing technology that is already developed there, bringing it back to this country under licensing agreement, doing the extensive research and development work that is necessary to get it through the regulatory processes here, and then marketing those compounds. So we significantly reduce the research and development risk by not trying to synthesize molecules. As a company, you can't choose whether or not to change, because a lot of things that cause change—increased competition, consumer demand, and the economy—are beyond our control. But what an organization can choose to do is *manage* the change and *lessen* the risk."

As Wheeler says, we can't always control the changes that confront us. But if you keep in pursuit of solutions to problems that arise from changes that confront you, you'll discover workable answers.

New Strategies for Developing a Corporate Mission Statement

To help employees and management stay on the same track, many companies write a corporate charter or mission statement based on their vision. Having the vision reduced to one or two sentences helps to clarify expectations. The charter helps the organization determine what business they *are* in and what business they *should* be in. Unfortunately, sometimes there is a huge difference. Is your company in the land development business but spending most of its working capital on investing in hotels overseas? My charter was to speak to groups; but when I studied the marketplace, I determined that I would fare better by making my charter more specific and moving into the one-day seminar business.

As discussed earlier, Home Federal reframed its mission statement from "order taking" to "sales and service." Adelizzi says, "One of the first things I ask myself each morning is, 'Are we tracking along the strategic guidelines set forth in our mission statement?'"

In 1985, Hospital Corporation of America restated its charter. In addition to owning and managing hospitals, the company acquired a hospital supply company and is now in the total health-care systems business. And Yamaha was in the business of making motorcycles when it expanded its charter to make beautifully tuned machines, including musical instruments.

Such diversification may be wise, or it may be the bane of the company if it's not carefully planned. Without periodically referring to the charter, a company may begin to strive for goals that are actually opposed to its original intent. Ask yourself how your product line fits in with your charter. And be willing to admit if something is a loser and needs to be extracted from your product line. Try to think of the up and down side of the changes the organization is contemplating, and be willing to ask yourself what the worst thing is that could happen to the organization if you make these changes—and what is the best way the company can benefit from them.

Keeping a Personal Journal to Chart the Progress of Change

Monitoring how changes in your company affect you on a personal level is also important. As Home Federal found out, organizations frequently outgrow employees who were competent during the early stages of the company's development, but who could not adjust to changes that occurred as the company matured. If you recognize early warning signals that tell you you're becoming frustrated and anxious, try to find solutions to your problems as soon as they begin developing and while others still have positive feelings about you and are eager to help.

To know how you are feeling when you are experiencing the discomfort of change or how you are feeling at any time in your life, you may want to keep a journal. You don't have to make daily entries; just be sure to write in your journal at significant times in your life. If you are going through a change, describe your feelings. Or, on your birthday or the anniversary of your employment, write down your goals for the upcoming year. Your journal will keep you in touch with concrete information about yourself rather than just impressions of how you feel. It will give you valuable data on what you like, when you feel depressed, what tasks are exciting to you and what you feel your strengths are.

I keep a journal of my own personal growth and development in my computer and make entries several times a week. When someone suggests how I might approach something differently, I make a note of it. I also record evaluations from speaking engagements and input reminders of areas I want to bone up on. My journal serves several purposes. It reminds me of areas in which I want to grow and change and it lets me see how far I've come. When I go back and reread entries from 15 years ago and see the issues I was struggling with then, I am able to see that I can overcome obstacles and I can change. It also gives me more compassion for what others are going through. Several months ago, for example, my son-in-law was having difficulties in business that I might have thought were trifling if I hadn't gone back and read about the troubles I had faced when I was his age. A journal can help you monitor all you've been through; it can show you that life is just a series of changes, and give you the perspective you need to move ahead.

Remember that your most dominant thought is the one that drives you, and the pictures you put in the photo album of your mind are the ones that influence how you live your life. Take time to examine the thoughts and pictures in your mind. Ask yourself if they are the ones that will serve you best today and if they are the vision you want for tomorrow. What makes the difference between mediocrity and greatness is the willingness to make adjustments, and the flexibility to incorporate new opportunities and responsibilities into our world view.

Yes, but...

Yes, but how can I find all this energy to solve problems when the problems themselves are an energy drain?

It's in the heat of need that we find inspiration for solutions to problems. For example, for two years the cotton crops in Enterprise, Alabama, were plagued by a boll weevil infestation that forced farmers to quit growing cotton and begin growing peanuts. Today, a statue to the boll weevil stands in Enterprise because it was the impetus that made them turn to peanuts, which have proven to be a much more lucrative source of income than cotton ever would have been. Enterprise farmers did not settle for living with their frustration. They actively pursued other alternatives.

Yes, I want to help my company weather changes, but I don't know how to monitor them.

Here are a few approaches to consider:

—Ask others for their honest input and try to ascertain whether you really are out of pace, and if so how much and why;

—Listen to others' suggestions for what you can do to change;

—Discuss the situation with a consultant to gain a different perspective;

—Read about how other companies have changed and what employees did to adapt to the new environment.

CHAPTER 3

Preserving the Valuable: Unearthing the Full Potential in Ourselves and Others

━━

You've seen it dozens of times. The leadership wants to rebuild or strengthen the company, so it takes a machete to layers of management and support personnel without considering the consequences of the sweeping cuts. Or a new manager runs through his department like a raving maniac, making snap judgments in an effort to turn the department around as quickly as possible. Before he gets a chance to fire anyone, the competent employees quit.

In our eagerness to revitalize a company or department, it sometimes seems easier to tear the existing structure down and start over than to salvage what we have. But while we may get rid of the workers who have been weighing us down, we may also be discarding unpolished gems who, with a little care and attention, could provide the quality and sparkle we value.

Russell Herman Conwell, founder of Temple University in Philadelphia, often told a powerful story about a diamond mine worker who dreamed one day of owning his own mine. The man saved and saved and finally decided to sell the property he owned to have a grub stake to quit his job and travel the country to discover a diamond mine. After decades of searching, the man returned to his home to discover that the property he used to own was now a thriving diamond mine. That fellow had diamonds in the rough all along. If he had just taken the time to unearth the potential of what he already had, his hopes and dreams could have been realized.

We often make the same mistake with people who work for us. Most of us want to believe that there is a simple answer to our troubles—that if we can just find the right people to do the job, our problems will be solved. Rather than carefully combing through personnel and considering the qualities of each individual, we tend to run roughshod through our department or company, perhaps burying several rough diamonds in pursuit of a single shiny jewel. This short-sighted mode of operation can cause long-range problems for the organization.

Rather than fire an entire department of employees or scrap existing equipment, we need to evaluate our perceptions of what our business should be and take a hard look at what we already have. Would firing Elroy be wise in the long run, or would investing time in his development be beneficial to him and the company? We need to take the time to recognize employees who are modestly valuable today, but who could be great contributors six months from now if enough energy were directed toward them.

Just as we know the importance of keeping the front door closed during the winter to conserve heat in our homes, we need to learn the value of holding onto and protecting the people, systems, equipment, and dreams that are contributing to a company's positive energy. True, we need to weed out those who are unproductive; but it's just as wasteful to get rid of someone or something that could have worked out as it is to make do with something that's not working.

That's not to say that we shouldn't own up to bad business decisions or that we shouldn't beware of overinvesting in long shots. Did you know that one of the main reasons hot air balloons crash is that people feel that they have invested so much in getting the balloon prepared that they try to go up even when the conditions aren't right?

I wrecked my plane once because I tried to salvage a bad landing approach. I was coming in a little too high and too fast with too much tail wind. Those three danger signs should have flashed a warning light in my mind. But in my determination to make the landing I ignored those indicators and the plane flipped. I would have saved my plane if only I had swallowed my pride and allowed myself to say, "I screwed up on this approach; I'll go around and try again." The same thing happens in an organization. We commit to a decision and don't want to admit that we've taken the wrong approach. Because we were stubborn and a little too proud, we crash and burn. You decide if it's worth it!

If I take a close look at what I can salvage in my company, I may see that the majority of my employees are working hard and contributing, and that only a few really need to be replaced. And instead of buying all new equipment, maybe I can network the equipment I have to enhance its capabilities. Then, what I've done is to discover the good that exists in what I have. I've preserved the valuable.

To develop a systems approach that allows us to explore where energy exists in our organization and avoid overlooking the valuable resources we have, we first need to examine our perceptions and distinguish between who and what we *think* is valuable and what is *really* valuable. What are the effectiveness indicators we use to judge performance? What does "valuable" look like in our organization? Is it working long hours? Or is it the ability to get things done or to meet customers' needs or to rack up sales?

For example, allowing employees to accept extra pay instead of taking their vacations or requiring them to work excessive amounts of overtime may appear valuable, but in reality it zaps their energy and effectiveness. Or, we may be so over-extended that we don't invest the time necessary to train and orient adequately new employees who come on board. They become so frustrated and confused that they jump ship.

We can also look at whether our management style stifles

the troops or excites them. Do we give employees credit and recognition? Or do we deny them positive feedback and put them down in an attempt to "manage?" Do we give our employees a realistic picture of what we expect and ask them for their input about our expectations? Often we ask employees to perform tasks that are impossible for them to do with the amount of support (budget and staff) that we've allotted them. Before we point the finger at our employees and blame them for the company's inefficiencies, it makes sense to look inwardly and determine if we are really giving enough—be it recognition or resources—to help them succeed. In other words, energetic managers accept responsibility before doling out blame.

Attention to the Present Pays Off in the Future

One of the first steps to hanging on to what you've got is learning to live in the present. Just like people who hop from one job or relationship to another, thinking that greener pastures lie elsewhere, some unhealthy businesses focus too much on past problems or put too much emphasis on "what could be." That's a normal reaction because it often seems easier and less painful to look backward or forward than to take a close look at where we are today. Self-examination takes place in the present; it is sometimes painful, but there is always a payoff.

One specific incident in my life taught me how living in the present allows the past and the future to serve us. Several years ago, one of my best friends was dying of cancer. At that time I was traveling a lot, so I would visit her about once every 10 days between business trips. One day I learned that my friend was much worse and was expected to die, so I hurried to see her. When I walked down the hospital corridor I was thinking in the present—even though I was aware of her past and knew what was expected in her future.

When I saw her I couldn't believe she had become so emaciated in such a brief period of time. The sight of her took my breath away—I couldn't talk and tears welled in my eyes. I thought I was going to have to leave the room. But then, I remembered what someone once told me: if I ever got caught up emotionally I should stop talking and start looking. So I looked as intently as I could into her eyes. In less than a minute my strength returned.

When I tried to understand why that worked, this is what I realized. I was living in the present when I walked into her room, but when I saw my friend's weakened state, my mind spun back to the past. I thought how the two of us used to play and go on picnics together with our families. The next moment, the future flooded my mind. I realized that the next time I saw my friend would probably be at her funeral. I learned that I can't deal with the present when 99 percent of me is caught up in the past and future. Locking eyes with her brought me back to the present. I was rewarded with the ability to be at her side and to experience the moment—something I'll never forget.

Does that sound like something that happens to you? Do you ever live in the past with regret and in the future with fear, and have little time for the present? While learning from the past and preparing for the future are key ingredients for success, the bulk of our energy should be spent on the here and now. For example, we may spend a lot of time discussing how to get a project completed by next week—when what we really need to look at is how effectively we're operating today. Or we may hold a meeting to plan a future event and ignore how we are using our energy during the meeting. Once you bring your activities into the present, you'll be amazed at how much better you'll be able to cope with a variety of situations.

Four Questions for Assessing Your Company's Strengths and Weaknesses

Before we make snap decisions that we think will improve business, it's important to take the pulse of the organization and see how energy is being used and misused. Is it the behavior of the entire organization that's causing problems, or are there a few specific people who seem to be thwarting success? What is really going wrong during department meetings that is making employees' spirits sag? And why did your relationship with a colleague suddenly sour?

Take a few minutes to make the following important observations:

—Are managers putting each other down and sabotaging each others' efforts?

—Do employees give each other immediate feedback or do problems build up and then explode?

—Are staff members willing to get involved in each other's problems and find solutions together, or does the "It's not my problem" attitude prevail?

—Is your organization built on feelings of trust and authenticity, or do employees worry about what others are really saying and thinking?

If you take time to assess your organization's strengths and weaknesses thoughtfully—rather than just acting on your preconceived assumptions and "snap" perceptions—the decisions you make will be more on target. You may want to seek the opinions and viewpoints of other people you trust. And you may see that you don't need to get rid of employees; you need to determine how to transform them into leaders—of their jobs and their lives.

How Company Leaders Can Encourage Team Spirit for That Winner's Edge

As you plan for a turnaround in your department or organization, don't forget to nurture those employees who have continued to contribute all along so that they will stay with you even through the rough times. To keep employees interested and involved during a transition period, it's important to keep them apprised of your goals on a regular basis. Give them something to dream about and work toward.

That's one of the reasons why Specialized Systems, Inc. (SSI), a company based in Carlsbad, California, was able to make such a dramatic turnaround. After eight years of marketing and repairing telecommunications devices for the deaf (TTDs), SSI realized that the demand for its products was limited—a fact reflected by the sagging profit margin. In an unorthodox attempt to right the situation, the company radically diverged from its original company charter and began silk-screening and marketing T-shirts and other sundry items such as bumper stickers and sweatshirts, along with selling the TTDs

Stephen Nemergut, J.D., president of SSI, had formed the company in 1977 to market a variety of products to consumers. But when SSI's role changed to a high-tech research and development company with little or no money spent on marketing and sales, he left. When the Board of Directors asked him to rejoin the company three years later, SSI sales had plummeted to $15,000 a month with expenses totaling $75,000 a month.

"I realized that we had a good product in the TTD but that we also had to get new business in here," says Nemergut. "For the first three months we concentrated on making the most of the TTD market while looking for new products. We had a warehouse full of TTDs that needed repairs, but no one was working on them because the company had become so lethargic. I saw that there was a market for repairing these devices and began preparing them for AT&T."

Within a few months, SSI's income rose from $20,000 to $60,000 a month just by taking advantage of the products it had in stock and motivating its staff.

"We told our employees and the sales representatives marketing the TTDs that things at SSI were going to change and that we were going to make money," recalls Nemergut. "We also let them know that we were looking for additional products to market. When management decided to begin silk-screening and marketing T-shirts, what came as a surprise was not the fact that we had new products and expected our people to produce and sell them, but the wide divergence in our product line."

Nemergut believes that a leader in an organization can create excitement about what the company is doing. He says the good employees—he calls them the "gems"—pick up on that excitement.

"With very little other motivation, they accept the enjoyment of seeing something that was not working, work," explains Nemergut. "The gems at SSI picked up very quickly on the state the company was in, rolled up their sleeves, and made what I think was a tremendous effort to work beyond their job descriptions. Others who couldn't or wouldn't respond were asked to leave. To those who stayed, it didn't matter if we were repairing and marketing TTDs or printing and selling T-shirts. What did matter was their commitment to making the company work."

Not only did SSI's gems roll up their sleeves, but at a moment's notice employees changed from business suits and skirts to tennies and T's. "At 10 a.m., if I said I needed someone to help with T-shirts, the office crew would slip into their jeans and head out to the back of the plant to help with the burgeoning silk-screening business," says George Coleman, chief operating officer. "When push came to shove, they were more interested in pitching in and helping the company than they were in saying, 'This is beneath me,' or 'My title doesn't call for this.' And this kind of response is rewarding."

June McClelland, administrative assistant, felt that management helped make the transition from TTD's into T-shirts easier because, "They provided us with guidelines and then allowed each of us to reach our own potential. By doing that they gave us the encouragement we needed to reach higher, and to strive beyond what we thought we could do."

And SSI's managers aren't sitting with their feet propped up on their desks delegating the company's drastic change in direction. "When we're needed, we are right out there working with employees, unpacking and pulling shirts for printing and preparing mailing labels," says Coleman. "This helps employees realize that we are all in this together."

When SSI began its T-shirt venture in March, 1985, sales were $70,000 to $100,000 a quarter. The first quarter of 1986, sales soared to approximately $600,000 or $700,000. For the next year, the sales projections were significantly higher. In one year, the T-shirts had virtually taken over SSI and now comprise 95 percent of the business.

When asked what the most important factor was to getting employees to support the transition, Coleman responds, "We made our employees feel that they were part of a team. Communications were open, not hidden. Employees knew exactly what was going on, what we were doing, and how we were doing it. There were no secrets, and they were told from the start that as the company grew, they would grow with it."

Adds Nemergut, "Management created a belief that employees are an integral part of the company, and that success had as much to do with them as it did with management."

And what do the gems at SSI think? Rhonda Heiple, 26, T-shirt control coordinator, joined SSI as a receptionist just before the company tried on the T-shirt venture. "Soon after we got into T-shirts, employees could sense a difference in the company," she says. "And when we saw how hard management was working to build the organization, it was easy to catch that feeling of excitement and get involved any way I could. To see T-shirt orders that previously took two weeks to process be ready to ship in two days is satisfying, and to know that you are a part of the progress is even more rewarding. Everyone is willing to put in the extra time because we know our contributions won't go unnoticed."

"All anybody here used to know about T-shirts was that we wore them on weekends," says Coleman. "Thanks to the enthusiasm of our employees, our new business is a perfect fit."

Just as SSI found a way to keep those employees who caught the spirit of their new business ventures, even if it meant retraining them or using them in different ways, many companies can benefit from keeping valuable employees excited about their work—even after years on the job. One of the surest ways to motivate employees is through recognition. The word *recognition* literally means "knowing again." It's re-seeing something familiar with fresh eyes and acknowledging it.

Often we get so caught up in working toward goals that we forget to recognize or celebrate accomplishments. To safeguard against this, some companies build celebration into their corporate culture. During its regular Friday get-together, in which management and employees informally discuss the week's events, Tandem Computers also sets aside time to recognize achievements. Managers announce employees' accomplishments and the entire company cheers—now that's a celebration!

Another way to keep the people we work with energized is always to imagine the consequences of what we think, do and say. Our natural tendency is to think of ourselves first. If I get upset at John and storm into his office before thinking things through, I may trigger an unnecessary argument. But instead of placing myself on top, I'd be better off thinking, "I wonder how John feels about this? I wonder if he needs more information. What can I do to help him? Will my comment dispirit him?" If I live my life like this rather than thinking only about myself, I will make investments in people and get the best return from them.

Any of us who are intent on energizing our department or organization knows that we don't have years to develop the essential attitudes of commitment and excitement in employees. So we must pay special attention to the hiring process and look for employees who will immediately be comfortable with the fact that in our organization, each employee is expected to be the leader of his or her own job. Once employees are on board, we must teach them to be strong advocates of their jobs, and be sure they get the tools they need to do their best. And we must strive to maintain the type of corporate culture where employees will be encouraged to act and react positively.

That means we must nurture the valuable by giving credit when it is due. When someone suggests an idea, we need to learn to accentuate the positive points of the idea, not dwell on the negative. In other words, we need to focus on people's strengths, not their weaknesses.

An important, but often overlooked, role of a manager is to help people preserve what they know. We can do that by remembering the four R's: Reiterate, Remind, Review, and Remember. Often it's the basic things we need to know that we have a tendency to forget. One of the greatest values of our seminars is that they help people preserve the wisdom they have. The reiteration and reinforcement remind them about what they do know. People are always telling me, "I'm glad you mentioned that point. I realize it's important, but I have forgotten to do it."

Helping Employees Size Up Their Strengths Can Avoid Business Misfits

When a company shifts gears, the leadership sometimes believes that long-term employees will be the most resistant to the changes, and determines to get rid of tenured employees and make a fresh start. But before we make that rash decision, why not determine whether we can transform those employees' thinking or use their talents in a new way? When the culture of an organization changes, positions must often change as well.

Two reasons many employees feel a lack of job satisfaction are that they either are not feeling challenged by their jobs or they do not feel prepared to accomplish the tasks set before them. Put more simply, they are not appropriately matched to their positions within the company. We may have a valuable person in the wrong position.

You may have a highly energetic employee who loves the steady, detailed work of accounting—but if you've put him on the fast track in a department like marketing, he may be unhappy. Or you may have someone who loves to be involved with people, and would shine in personnel, pent up in data processing where the only interaction is with the beams and beeps of the computer screen. These employees are frustrated and dissatisfied because they are spending the majority of their energy trying to compensate for their weaknesses, rather than optimizing and capitalizing on their strengths.

We spend too much time trying to be all things to all people. We chastise ourselves with comments like, "I really ought to do this," or "I should have done that," rather than working in an environment that makes the best use of our talents. Here's a parable that points to the familiar frustration of trying to do everything well and not concentrating on perfecting our natural talents. Once upon a time, the animal kingdom decided to do something meaningful to help solve the world's problems, and to "cross-train" its members. It organized a school and adopted an activity curriculum of running, climbing, swimming, and flying. To make it easier to administer the curriculum, each animal was required to take and pass all the available subjects to graduate.

The duck was an excellent swimmer, but made only passing grades in flying, and almost failed at running. Since he was a slow runner, he had to stay after school to practice. His webbed feet become so badly worn that he dropped to an average in his swimming class. But average was quite acceptable, so nobody worried about his performance—except the duck.

The rabbit quickly jumped to the top of the class in running but soon developed a nervous twitch in his leg muscles from the makeup work he had to do in swimming class.

The squirrel excelled in climbing, but encountered constant frustration studying flying because the teacher made him work from the ground up instead of from the top down. He developed charley horses from overexertion and received a "C" in climbing and a "D" in running.

The eagle was a problem student in all his classes and was severely disciplined for being a nonconformist. In climbing, he beat all the others to the top of the tree, but insisted on using his own means of getting there instead of following the instructions outlined in the textbook.

Each creature in the animal kingdom has its own set of capabilities at which it naturally excels. A duck is a duck. It's built to swim; not to run. If it's forced into a mold that does not fit, frustration and disappointment ensue and mediocrity and defeat often result.

Brad Loehr, 24, used to work in the electronics division for SSI, but when the silk-screening process began, management noticed that his interests were suddenly diverted. "I was really interested in electronics, but the work I was doing was tedious and monotonous," says Loehr. "Silk screening really caught my eye, and I began reading magazine articles about it and was surprised to learn how really technical the process gets."

When things in his department got slow, Loehr, like all SSI employees, was asked to help out with T-shirts. Finally Coleman noticed how much Loehr had learned and asked him if he'd like to transfer to the printing department.

"I've never really worked at a job I truly loved," says Loehr. "Silk-screening is great, and I can't seem to get enough of it."

Loehr is in his element. Management now has to watch that Loehr doesn't work too much. "There have been many evenings that I've stayed late—on my own time—just to make sure I'll be prepared for the morning," says Loehr. "My job seems more like a hobby than work. Everyone here gets along so well, we're always willing to help each other out. Compared to other places I've worked at, I feel like I'm in a dreamland." (Loehr is now a supervisor in the silkscreen department.)

Wouldn't it be nice if all our employees felt like that?

Yes, but . . .

If you're still not convinced that trying to preserve as much as possible of what we have pays off, let me try once more. Are you saying to yourself:

—Yes, but I've always felt that if something didn't work, it was more efficient to get rid of it and start over.

Starting from scratch pays off sometimes, but before we make sweeping changes, we should slow down and take time to evaluate what we have so that we don't throw the baby out with the bath water. There's an old legend about a man who was given the ability to discover magic stones which at a touch would turn metal into gold. The man was told that he could find the magic stone on the shore's edge. But when he went to look, he found that the beach was covered with stones. To avoid picking up the same stones over and over again, he put a metal bracelet on his arm. If he picked up the magic stone and touched it to the bracelet, it would turn to gold. The man worked for hours picking up stone after stone, touching each to the bracelet and throwing it into the ocean if it didn't have the Midas touch. In his hurry to find the magic stone, he worked faster and faster. Soon his actions became routine—pick up, touch, look, toss. Pick up, touch, look, toss. Suddenly he looked at his bracelet and discovered that it had turned to gold, and he had already thrown the stone into the sea. Sometimes in our haste, we, too, throw away the valuable.

—Yes, but do all those "warm fuzzies" you talk about to keep employees energized really pay off?

As your company makes the transition from one that has been idling in neutral to a truly energized organization about to take off, more and more demands will be put on employees. If you don't balance the demands with recognition, employees may begin to resent management's decisions.

Let me illustrate this with a simple exercise. Place your hands together. Push your left hand with your right. Did you automatically push back with your left hand—even though that wasn't part of the instructions?

That happens in business too. If employees feel that management is pushing too hard, it's natural for them to push back. They may start procrastinating and not working as hard as they could. Experience has shown me that the more positive reinforcement I give my employees, the more cooperative and effective they are.

HERE REPLACEMENS BEFORE
DISMISSING EMPLOYEE.

CHAPTER 4

Beating the Blues:
Identify and Eliminate
Your Emotional Saboteurs

Scientists believe that a "black hole" lies at the center of the Milky Way, actively devouring galactic matter. It's thought that when the galaxy was formed, an agglomeration of stars, dust and gas collected at its center. This material's gravitational pull was so strong that it collapsed inward. The original matter disappeared—but the gravitational pull continued to gobble up stars and dust.

That theory sounds plausible to me. In fact, I've known black holes to eat away at me and those I work with. Creative ideas, positive attitudes, and cooperative spirits have been snatched out of our grip by some unexplainable force. It's as though a black hole steals our energy.

As a manager, do you ever fall prey to black holes, those frightening energy bandits—pessimism, worry, fear, backbiting, and defensiveness—that hold up your good intentions and hijack your effectiveness? Some energy robbers, like anger and complaining, are blatant and easy to identify. But more subtle and subversive energy thieves such as apathy, daydreaming and lack of interest, can swipe positive feelings, without anyone's really knowing why.

One especially elusive energy robber is the wasting of resources—like time, money or supplies. Imagine the nightmare of sending out a mailing of 2,000 brochures to your potential clients, only to have a fourth of them returned for lack of a good address. Checking the mailing list you realize no one has bothered to update it for months. You'll really wish you were dreaming when you have to justify the expense of redoing the mailing.

Can you think of any instances where the energy in your department or company has been misdirected or diffused, and work thus rendered useless? What are the black holes that are draining life from you, your employees, your department, your family? You'll defend yourself better against these thieves of good spirits and productivity if you can determine when you are most vulnerable to a siege, how to outwit energy ambushes, and how to arm yourself against a possible attack.

Unlearning Self-Obstructive Behaviors: Fighting Back When You Are Your Own Worst Enemy

I'm convinced that the most heavily armed and dangerous energy robber is the SOB. What I'm talking about is the Self-Obstructing Behavior we do to ourselves. SOBs are self-defeating put-downs and negative inner dialogues that make us question our worth and inhibit our performance.

For example, what good comes from performing 99 percent of a job well, if we feel incompetent because the remaining 1 percent doesn't meet our standards? What are the roadblocks you construct for yourself that make your thoughts and actions take a negative detour? Do you constantly worry, complain, gripe or belittle yourself in your mind or in front of others? Or do you try to camouflage insecurities by bragging, acting defensive, or berating others?

A lot of successful people are harder on themselves than they are on others. But when we call ourselves names like "stupid" or "ineffective," or when we constantly berate ourselves and dwell on our mistakes, it's the same as saying, "I'm guilty." The adage "You are what you have been becoming" reinforces the point that how we act and react each day has a profound effect on who we are today and who we will be tomorrow.

Several years ago in Philadelphia I heard about an accident in the bumper-to-bumper traffic on one of the city's freeways. A driver stopped abruptly and was rear-ended. The driver of the first vehicle stormed out of his car and began verbally attacking the other driver. Suddenly the driver of the second car pulled out a .45 and shot and killed the first man.

My guess is that the man who became irate and was shot had probably lost his cool on many occasions. Most likely he started practicing his dictatorial and irrational behavior with his wife and kids, then at work, and finally with strangers, until he was ready for the grand finale on the freeway.

Is it possible that you're practicing an attitude or outlook right now that will eventually do you in? Many of us have a tendency to live like time bombs just waiting for something to set us off. That's why it's so important to spend some time and energy working on eliminating those detonating SOBs from our lives. Defusing the SOBs will give you the self-assurance and confidence that remind you, "I'm a good person."

But putting the SOBs behind bars isn't enough to assure contentment and success. Not only must we deal with the bad in our lives, we must nourish the good as well. Just as we must eat nutritious foods to perform optimally, we also need to give and receive healthy emotional groceries if we want to feel satisfied personally and work well with others. Negative emotions affect our body as well as our mind. Did you know that when we panic our blood vessels constrict, limiting the supply of oxygen to our body? Every time we get worked up about what we ought to do, should do, or must do, we create feelings of failure instead of success—dissonance rather than harmony—and we concentrate on how far away we are from our goal now instead of how close.

On the flip side, positive emotions energize us and give us a sense of well-being because, as Norman Cousins has pointed out, they are thought to release endorphins—nature's opiates—from our brain, just as they are thought to do in runners. In fact, Cousins told me that it was the stress—all the "have-tos" in his life—that had caused his heart attack.

He had been traveling so much that he asked his secretary to see if he could get out of attending an engagement. The secretary checked into it and reported that, unless there was just no way he could attend, he would need to keep the appointment. Cousins believes that he could subconsciously have "caused" the heart attack as a way to get the break he needed. We may not give ourselves heart attacks, but in subtle ways we often booby-trap our well-being.

As Cousins recovered from his heart attack, he used laughter (as he had used it to combat an earlier serious illness)—among many other things—to help grow stronger. Like Cousins, I think we'd all benefit if we could learn to add levity to our lives and find a way to joke about our problems. As he has noted in his writings and lectures, laughter enlarges our blood vessels, releases endorphins, and allows us to cope with life's large and small problems more effectively. In our office at Pryor Resources, Inc. we have a couple of people who periodically burst into laughter spontaneously, and their laughter helps relieve tension in the entire office. We've found that it's pretty cheap therapy to encourage others to share their senses of humor and make everybody feel good.

But don't expect yourself to be upbeat all the time. If you can't make light of a mistake you have made, do something healthy to get your mind off what you're doing. Absorbing activities such as sports and music are some of the best cures for tension and frustration, and are certainly better than washing problems away with booze or dissolving them with an hourly antacid. Keep your body working for you, not against you.

Another way to eradicate the SOBs from your life is to focus on eliminating one per week. The first week, decide to stop saying "I can't." (When it's used often enough, that type of statement becomes a self-fulfilling prophecy and threatens to squelch our ability and creativity.) The second week, work on erasing other negative self-talk tapes, including such statements as "I'm not that talented" or "I can't believe I'm so stupid."Try to catch yourself in the midst of an SOB and don't allow yourself to continue. You may even want to ask a friend or colleague to work on his or her attitude at the same time. Blow the whistle on each other, and compare notes at the end of the week to see how you've improved.

And while you're working to eliminate SOBs from your life, don't let others get away with cutting remarks or subtle digs. Remember that it is your responsibility to keep yourself in good mental condition and to know how to handle the attacks of others. As Eleanor Roosevelt once said, "No one can make you feel inferior without your consent." (*This Is My Story*, Harper and Brothers, 1937.)

If you feed yourself positive emotional groceries, celebrate your accomplishments, and try to surround yourself with other people who support you, you'll have the sustenance that will keep you mentally strong. When someone tries to put you down, your healthy attitude will put you in good shape to fight back. And if someone pulls a punch, don't let it go unnoticed. Let the person know how you feel about his or her aggression by saying something like, "It really bothers me when you make comments like that. What can we do to iron out our differences?"

Sporting a New Attitude:
How to Turn Vicious Game Playing
into Productive Teamwork

People find it difficult to address problems directly, so instead they develop behaviors and ploys that allow them to evade the issue. These "games" run the gamut from "Poor me—" feeling sorry for yourself because something didn't go your way and deciding not to join in other activities—to pitting one department against another to prove your own superiority. But such behaviors only lead to ill feelings, and petty complaints, or provide grist for the rumor mill, which severely hampers productivity. And if we're not careful, the games people play can turn serious—becoming legitimized over time until they actually become a way of life.

To keep from getting coaxed into such games, be aware of the tactics people use to lure others. Then, make a conscious decision not to be persuaded to take part. Conducting an honest appraisal of our interactions with others will help us determine if we are playing games, as will asking others to point out when we are falling into the trap.

No matter how perceptive we are at noticing the games other people engage in, it's easy to have blind spots when it comes to owning up to our own antics. One way to get an accurate image of ourselves is to ask a few close colleagues to act as our mirrors and reflect our good points as well as those that need improvement. Others may see facades we put up that, if stripped off, would improve our effectiveness. Getting a glimpse of our entire image—what others see as well as what we try to project—helps to foster growth and development and makes us less likely to repeat errors that are masked by our blind spots.

Sometimes, as managers, we want our department or company to run so smoothly that we actually ignore or explain away justified concerns our employees might have about a particular employee's performance. Realize that there can be times when you get so caught up in what you're doing that you don't see things as they actually are. If you build a support system of people you can trust who will provide you with honest feedback—and then listen to what they have to say—you will gain the perspective you need.

Let the Momentum of Change
Propel You Toward Your Goals

Just as it's important to become pro-change in order to "vision" the future we desire (as I have pointed out in Chapter

2), it's also important to learn to embrace—and not resist—change in order to overcome negative energy. Seeing change as something threatening may mean that we don't buy the new equipment, adapt the new technology, or employ the new system that will save us time and resources. Remember the saying, "We can only accomplish what we first imagine." If we can picture ourselves working cooperatively with new procedures or new corporate leaders, we'll be a lot closer to achieving these goals.

That philosophy is at the heart of the Greek myth about Pygmalion, a sculptor who had a picture in his mind of a beautiful woman, but couldn't find anyone who matched that vision. Finally he decided to sculpt her image. He created such a flawless figure that he grew more frustrated that he couldn't find a living woman who could match this figment of his imagination. Sympathizing with the difficulty Pygmalion was having, the gods took pity and breathed life into the statue, making his dream a reality.

I think this story is still told today because most of us realize that there is a kernel of truth in the Pygmalion phenomenon. We know that we can make some things come true simply by believing in them. Having a positive attitude toward issues helps us deal effectively with them and create positive experiences. Taking a defeatist attitude such as "I just know I'm going to blow it" often becomes a self-fulfilling prophesy.

Taken one step further, if I heap doubt on John in my department—telling him that I don't think he has what it takes to do the job—my lack of confidence is likely to infect him. If I act as if I expect him to fail, he probably will. But if I have a positive Pygmalion attitude toward John, he'll pick up on it and be much more disposed toward success. Even if I don't consistently let him know how I feel about his contributions, John will be able to tell by my nonverbal communication of support—which often speaks louder than words.

We can't separate our attitudes from ourselves or from how we act, react, or interact. A negative attitude toward one issue can easily become the focal point of our lives. If we're not careful, it can become generalized to other areas—and eventually become so magnified that we don't like ourself or anyone or anything else.

The kind of thoughts you have are the raw materials with which you build your character. They house the way you feel and construct others' opinions about you. You can live with a mind that is a dilapidated shack or one that is a sparkling, spacious mansion. The choice is yours. I'm not suggesting that you stand in front of a mirror and chant endless self-praise. But realize that you are the master of your own fate.

There is no hocus-pocus to making positive changes in your life. Start by making a list of what you want to change, and talk to others who have been successful in overcoming their troubles. One of the reasons I believe Alcoholics Anonymous is successful is that members are able to pull each other through the rough spots by offering nonjudgmental support because "they've been there."

While I was speaking about managing stress at a meeting of the Young Presidents Organization in Durango, Colorado, Richard Hojel, the president of a large company, told me about a tragic incident in his life that taught him it is possible to face and endure crises. One of his children accidentally released a helium balloon, and it got stuck in the powerline in front of their home. Hojel got his golf ball retriever and went up on the second floor balcony to fetch the balloon. He leaned over the balcony, held onto the weather vane, and just as he was pulling in the balloon, a high voltage line backsurged. The bolt of electricity completely charred his hands before throwing him 40 feet, and even melted the metal weather vane. Ultimately he lost both hands.

Hojel told me that during his recuperation, he felt like a mere shadow of his former self. He was so afraid people would shy away from him because of his handicap and disfigurement that when anyone asked how he was doing he always said, "I'm fine." After continually insisting that he felt fine, Hojel actually started feeling fine. In other words, he talked himself into being well.

Hojel has been an inspiration to me. If anybody had reason to be bitter and complain, he certainly did. But instead he reinforced the fact that reality is not *what* happens to us, but what our mind *thinks* about what happens. If how you think is powerful enough to shape your reality, imagine the impact positive thinking could have on your life! What I'm suggesting is that if you and I really want to be on top of our lives and businesses, we have to elevate our way of thinking.

Meet Employees' Needs and They Will Serve You Well

As company leaders, we manage other people's workdays, and our attitudes create the type of environment our staff members inhabit during one-third of their lives. It's our job to offer employees a place to work where they can flourish, develop, and grow. Psychologists are finding that people are born with an innate talent to learn to do things right. But we unlearn this ability because our school system and society emphasize what we can't do rather than what we do well. Motivating employees to do their best is like cultivating a flower. If the flower is small and you want to make it bigger, you can't just yank on the stem hoping to stretch it. Instead, you need to enhance its environment by watering and feeding it. If you give it the right kind and proper amount of attention, the flower is more likely to grow and meet your expectations.

To help employees grow and change to meet our needs and the needs of the organization, we must be willing to provide the necessary care. Just as a plant will shoot its leaves toward the sunlight, people gravitate toward places where they get their needs met. As managers we need to help our employees see the light. When they realize that they get their needs met by working with us, employees blossom.

It's also our job to conduct employees away from negative energy, switching off comments like, "I don't know why this company has to be like this," or "This department has the dumbest systems I've ever seen." Instead of letting your staff short-circuit their energy by complaining among themselves, encourage them to air their feelings openly, assuring them that you want them to feel good about what they do. Then, be willing to determine adjustments that can be made within their jobs and their departments that will help them develop a positive attitude. One of the nicest parts of all of this is that the degree to which we give others what they need is the same degree to which they will meet our needs.

Anger Is Fear in Sheep's Clothing

I always thought that anger was a reaction to what someone else had done to me. But the day before I was to give one of my first seminars, I finally began to understand what anger really is. I checked into the hotel and immediately went to take a look at the conference room where I'd be speaking. The room was only half the size it needed to be and was set up with chairs and no tables. I quickly cornered the housekeeper and told him I had to have tables. When he explained that the hotel didn't have tables, I told him what he could do with his crummy chairs, the hotel, and everything else. Back in my room, I realized the reason I had gotten mad was that I was afraid not enough people would show up at the seminar. If I had taken time to cool down before yelling at the housekeeper, I would have recognized my fear and avoided making a scene. And if I had dealt more responsibly with my anger, I could have also avoided the resultant guilt.

The next time you get angry, ask yourself what you're afraid of. Then realize that much of what we fear is really the exaggerations of our imagination. You can enlarge your fear or you can reduce it. One of the best ways to conquer fear is to move toward it. For example, if you're afraid of flying, you may actually want to take part in a simulated flight exercise to learn to feel comfortable flying rather than spending the rest of your life traveling by train. Or you can talk to a professional who can help you determine why you fear flying and learn how to face it.

Moving toward fear may also mean making changes that you've been putting off or ignoring. You may need to terminate the employee who is a chronic complainer, for example, or sell the four-wheel drive truck that's devouring your bank account.

Worrying: It Gnaws Away at Creativity

Worrying is a another energy zapper—but unlike anger, which is blatant and brash, worrying does damage slowly and silently. The word "worry" is derived from the Dutch word "worgen," which means to throttle or strangle. That's appropriate, because if it's uncontrolled, worry has a way of choking out creativity, spontaneity, and productivity.

It has been said that in California there is the ruin of a gigantic redwood tree that has stood for hundreds of years, surviving everything from lightning strikes to avalanches and hurricane winds that uprooted neighboring trees. The mighty redwood finally met its match when an army of tiny beetles ate their way through its bark, gradually destroying the tree's inner strength and leveling it. Massive forces were not able to destroy the tree; but the slow accumulation of a smaller force—the beetles—was.

The same holds true for people. While we are able to cope with financial disasters, the death of loved ones, and devastating illnesses, we let the nitty-gritty of life eat away at us a little at a time. We tend to become preoccupied with the small items and let them keep us from putting our energy where it's really needed.

Director, Prima Donna, Understudy— Cast Yourself for Rave Reviews

My experience working with people in my own organization and as a consultant to others has led me to see that people typically approach life in one of three ways. If all the world's a stage, here are the distinct roles we can choose to play: understudy, prima donna or director. As I describe this trio, audition yourself to determine where you fit and where you'd like to be. *Are You an Understudy in Your Own Life?* Have you ever known someone who seems to be an understudy of his or her own life? That's the kind of person who is always waiting in the wings to go on stage—hoping for that big break but taking no steps to make the break happen. Unfortunately, I spent too many years of my own life being an understudy. I wished I could do things that other people were doing, but I thought that even if I could, I wouldn't do those things as well as they did. I'd find myself agreeing with people I didn't even understand. And if you think that's bad, sometimes I'd agree with two people who adamantly disagreed with each other! That type of approach to life kept me from succeeding in ways I wanted to.

Do you have any areas of your life in which you're an understudy? There may be some areas in which you are very interactive, but others in which you find yourself just sitting back passively letting life happen to you. For instance, you may be reading this book saying, "O.K. Fred, tell me something smart. Teach me something." You may think that since I'm the author I'm responsible for what you learn from this book. But I'd like to suggest that you really won't get what you deserve out of this book, or out of a seminar or any other body of information, unless you are totally in charge of your life.

One of the sad things I look back on in my life is the realization that I wasn't as actively involved in the development of my two daughters as I could have been. I was always intending to be a better father later. As soon as I had more time, I was going to play with them more and listen to them more intently. In that situation I was an understudy, and just thinking about it saps my energy. It's a treadmill existence and pretty soon, one day leads to another and you've made a life out of that same old pattern.

Are You a Legend in Your Own Mind? There's another kind of existence that is also a liability—that of the prima donna. The kind of person who is always singing self-praises, "me, me, me" and "I, I, I."

Do you ever find yourself getting sick of hearing such solos from some people? If you do, chances are it's because their stories seem calculated to let others know how great they are. It's as though they're legends in their own minds. They tell you about all their achievements and accomplishments, who they know, where they've been, and what they've done. And they seem to only respond to one way of doing things—their way. Whenever possible, they pull rank or authority to get what they want. After you've finished talking to someone like that, you realize that what has taken place was not a dialogue but a monologue, with only one person's goals and intentions in mind.

One statement I heard that helped me put the prima donna personality in perspective is: "When someone brags, you can be sure of one thing—they don't believe a word they say." That's because if people really believe they're highly competent, they have absolutely no need to plead their case. So when I find myself eager to tell someone why I'm right or important, I remember that type of behavior does not encourage people to work *with* me, it pushes them away. If I'm the type of person who has to have all the attention focused on me, I don't empower or facilitate others. And I certainly don't energize them.

Do You Take Charge of Your Life? I believe that the most rewarding way to live is to be a director of our own lives. To be in charge of who we are. And to be responsible for what we do, as well as what we do right. When we direct our lives, we don't blame, pass the buck, or complain. Instead we advocate our position and take charge of what happens to us.

Being a director does not, however, mean taking charge of other people's lives. Our ultimate goal is to encourage others to be directors of their lives, as well. That means that we have to think in new paradigms. We have to throw out old patterns— such as the classical one of the autocratic, dictatorial, domineering manager who tells others what they ought to, should, or must do.

It's hard to throw out the old pattern because many of us grew up in an autocratic family environment. But we'd never act that way with *our* kids—would we? I'm sure *we'd* never say something like, "Sit down, shut up, and listen," or "There you go again, what's wrong with you?" Maybe our neighbors act like that, but we certainly don't.

We have to be careful when we act like the autocrat around our children. Have you heard the story of the father who came home one evening to find his son lying in front of the television?

A warm glow shone around his son's head and the father thought to himself, "Abe Lincoln had a warm glow around his head, but it sure wasn't television, it was candlelight." He was reading—preparing for the future." Then the father chided his son, "Do you know what Abe Lincoln was doing when he was your age?" The kid thought for a moment and said, "No, Dad, but wasn't he President when he was *your* age?"

If you were raised by autocratic parents, you know it is not the most pleasant—or for that matter the most effective—method of operation. The same holds true for working in an autocratic environment. The old approach—namely, trying to control employees—worked for years because the boss controlled the workers, and they, in turn, controlled the equipment. But suddenly three-quarters of our culture is involved in the service industry. So now, if as the boss and role model, I control the employees, they will turn around and act in a controlling way to the customer. If someone says, "I'd like some help," the controlling employee responds with, "Well, what do you want and why didn't you ask sooner?" Or, "Don't complain to me, I've got enough problems of my own." That's called ineffective customer relations and it's one of the biggest energy robbers a business can have.

Managers today are learning to shift their thinking away from controlling employees to interfacing with them. Like a good theatrical director good managers provide their staffs with the direction and resources they need to get the job done. They encourage employees to move away from thinking like an understudy—assuming that they need to be told exactly what to do and when to do it—and from the self-absorbed, prima donna attitude, or the belief that we have to do it on our own without asking for support. They champion an interactive approach built on teamwork. Employees cooperate rather than compete for the spotlight, and the synergy that results from sharing ideas and resources propels the company forward. The ultimate result? Everyone wins—the manager because he or she is able to move the department or organization more quickly and efficiently toward its goal, and the employees because their confidence has been bolstered.

But does all this talk mean that employees should not be held responsible for their actions or be expected to think on their own? On the contrary. In an environment built on participation, employees feel more compelled than ever to take an interest in the company and in their personal growth. In fact, they are spurred on by the energy they feel emanating from others.

In an organizational environment where employees are only asked to do their job and nothing more, boredom sets in. Workers memorize their jobs the way an actor memorizes lines. But instead of feeling like a star, they feel like an understudy waiting for a big break—they're either waiting for someone in the position above them to quit, or waiting for the department manager to "discover" their talent.

I like to think that the most satisfied employees are directors of their own lives—those who take charge rather than letting life happen to them. They use all their resources and willingly ask for and give assistance, making the entire company's performance worthy of rave reviews.

I don't think any of us will win if we are prima donnas or understudies. Businesses today are giving employees more and more authority, so that it is more possible than ever to make our own breaks and become our own director. Becoming the director of your life means putting yourself in charge of what happens to you.

Here's an acronym that spells out the attributes of employers and employees who perform their jobs as DIRECTORS.

- D—Delegate. In addition to delegating to others, learn to delegate to yourself. Take responsibility and authority for what you do and hold yourself accountable.

- I—Inner Custodian. It's your job to keep yourself in shape emotionally and physically. Learn to listen to yourself and develop a sixth sense—an intuition—that will help you make smarter decisions.

- R—Risk. Live your life entrepreneurially. Learn to take risks and look for opportunities for personal growth. Confront issues instead of ignoring them.
- E—Empower. To have power is defined as "to be able." Develop an "I can" attitude to empower yourself, and help to motivate, not intimidate, other people in order to empower them.
- C—Celebrate. Take time to step away from your work, and celebrate your accomplishments and those of others.
- T—Test. Constantly put yourself to the test. Accept challenges and develop a sense of discipline.
- O—Optimize. Think of the *best* that can happen to you instead of dwelling on the negative. You'll increase your energy by telling yourself that you are capable of succeeding. With that kind of attitude you'll be much more in charge and in control.
- R—Radically present. Are you radically present or radically preoccupied? Wisdom comes from paying attention. Keep your life in balance so you can concentrate on work when you're at work and on your family when you're at home.

Here's a more in-depth explanation of what we can each do to become the director of our lives.

The "D" for Delegation is important because we often spend so much time worrying about what we have to get done that we forget to delegate—to others and to ourselves. Delegation means giving responsibility and authority and believing in the capabilities of those we delegate to.

More importantly, it means delegating to ourselves and holding ourselves accountable. Even though we expect our employees to account for what they do, we don't ask that much of ourselves! Think of what happens every New Year's. We make resolutions to stop a certain behavior, but by mid-January we let ourselves backslide and cast the resolution aside with the excuse, "I know I wouldn't be able to keep it anyway." But if you don't hold yourself accountable, you can't take charge of your life.

I try to live by the prayer, "Lord, let me live as long as I'm alive." To me that means that our journey—our day-to-day activities—needs to be our destination. I need to live my life with a sense of fulfillment each day. It's the director, not the understudy or prima donna, who is truly able to find satisfaction in each day.

The "I" in the acronym represents "Inner Custodian." That means that we keep our lives in order—making sweeping changes when they're needed. It means taking care of ourselves and finding creative ways to do so. There's a current saying, "Grow or die." It's a stark thought, but it's reality. Physically and mentally we have to care for ourselves. Today, we have a lot to say about the quality and quantity of our days, but most people are not thoroughly convinced of that. They still think they are going to "catch" a cold, "get" a coronary, or "come down with" some other type of illness. They act as though there were absolutely nothing they could do about what happens to them. The trouble with the Epicurean philosophy of "Eat, drink, and be merry, for tomorrow you may die," is that you don't die tomorrow. To get some perspective on why this may be a problem, spend a few hours in a nursing home. While some of the diseases people suffer from are uncontrollable, there are still many people in nursing homes who are living years of their lives in a meaningless, purposeless existence because they didn't plan while they still had the control. If you want to live as a director, you have to recognize that you are responsible for the inner-custodial care of your life.

The "R" stands for Risk. I know that you've probably already read a lot about the entrepreneurial spirit. You may even feel like the American businessman who, along with a Frenchman and Japanese, was given one last wish before he died. The Frenchman asked to address an audience at the Arc de Triomphe. The Japanese wanted to talk to people about quality circles. And the American said, "I'd like to be shot right now, because I don't think I can stand to hear one more talk on quality circles."

I hope you don't feel that way about what I have to say about living your life entrepreneurially. Entrepreneurs are risk-takers. In other words, they spend their lives looking for ways to be all they can. Do you realize that there are people who live enormously lonely lives simply because they're unwilling to risk their egos by telling someone, "I like you?"

Some people are afraid to confront issues. In fact, they'd rather live with the agony of a problem for many years than face the problem and encounter momentary pain or frustration. And you really don't need to feel pain if you approach problems the right way—by attacking the issue, not the person. If you let your feelings be known and ask for feedback, by saying something like, "I'm really disturbed by this. Can you help me understand what happened?" You can solve problems instead of letting them enlarge to the point of explosion.

Learning to take a risk doesn't mean you have to acquire new skills, because as a manager you already have most of the skills you need. Simply remember that they are only at your disposal if you are daring enough to call on them and put them to use.

The "E" in DIRECTOR represents Empowerment.
There's a Greek word for "power," *dynamis*, from which we get English words like "dynamite" and "dynamic." With that in mind, think of the dynamic energy you'll have if you empower yourself, if you put yourself in charge. And all the while, remember that what you think is how you feel.

If you can do that, you will have a frame of reference that will allow you to endure difficult circumstances and come away from them feeling strengthened rather than weakened. And you'll have the energy to empower others as well, motivating them rather than managing by intimidation.

The "C" represents Celebration. That's an area I need to work on in my life. I tend not to celebrate after an accomplishment but instead go right on to what I should do next. That's the mark of a perfectionist. The closer I get to my goal, the higher I push the goal. And if we continue to do that, chances are we'll die failures.

What we need to do is to stop and celebrate what we *have* done—and help others celebrate their accomplishments as well. Management by walking around, a concept mentioned in the book

In Search of Excellence, by Peters and Waterman (Harper & Row, 1982), has gotten a lot of positive press. But let's not just walk around to look involved. Let's actually take a few minutes and talk to our staff about what they've done that's good. And if they know we feel satisfied with their work, chances are they'll work even harder than they would if we just told them what aspects of their work disappointed us.

The "T" stands for Testing, testing yourself, that is. As the director of your life, you need to constantly put yourself to the test. You ask yourself questions like, "How do I face change?" "Do I readily accept new challenges?"

Most people resist change because it implies that they will have to do things in a new and different way. They know that it will take a lot of energy and effort to rethink how they do things, and they are already behind in their work.

When we test ourselves, we have the discipline to see the opportunities in the midst of the challenge. I don't want to be sickeningly optimistic and tell you, "You don't have problems, you have opportunities," but I do want to advocate the idea that such tests might bring out the best in us. It's interesting to me that as we grow older, we become less and less interested in testing ourselves because we dwell on our failures. But I hope that we will never be so pessimistic that we can't accept new challenges, because to me that's one of the best ways we obtain new energy.

The "O" means Optimism. You're not likely to do a very good job of leading yourself or anyone else if you put yourself down. Comments such as "I doubt that's going to work," "Today's probably going to be a bad day," or "I bet we're going to have a problem with the new person we hired," drain energy.

Rather than just moralizing, be optimistic. Develop anchors of hope such as good friends and good resources. Having these things to fall back on will give you more options, more hope, and more reasons to be optimistic.

Instead of allowing mismanaged stress to smother your energy, give yourself positive messages. Tell yourself, "I am a capable, competent person." "I make some mistakes, but that is an inevitable part of life." "I am effective and I see an opportunity to move forward." With that kind of attitude, you'll be much more in charge and will be perceived by others as being in control.

Finally, the "R" is to remind us to be "Radically Present." I like that because to me many of us are radically preoccupied. Have you ever talked to someone and wondered if "the lights were on but no one was home"?

Concentration is one of our greatest assets. But sometimes people talk to us and we really don't listen. In fact, it's been said that before a person commits suicide, he tells at least ten people. Some of us have been one of those ten people but we have not listened with the "third ear," which as Theodore Reik describes in his book *Listening with the Third Ear: The Inner Experience of a Psychoanalyst*, (Arena Books, 1975) means listening with meaning and purpose.

One of the secrets to managing our time is learning how to concentrate. For example, often we don't concentrate on what someone is saying to us, and our mind roams. That may mean that it takes much longer than necessary to get to the heart of the issue and for the other person to get what he or she needs from us. If we're not careful, we can develop a lifestyle like that in which we are not really present at work or at home. We may end up stealing time and opportunities from others and ourselves.

I think that all of us would like to develop the attributes of a director. We don't have to lead our lives as an understudy or prima donna. We can decide today to put our name on the back of that director's chair. And if we impart this type of thinking to those with whom we live and work, chances are we'll find that all our employees are infinitely happier individually, and collectively much more powerful, when they feel in control of their performance. And we'll reap the benefits of working with people with positive attitudes. These employees will no longer bow to the sour reviews of their SOBs—but will dwell on the positive applause they give themselves and others, as they struggle through tryouts and rehearsals and finally bask in the spotlight of a stellar performance.

Yes, but . . .

—Yes, I want to encourage my employees to become directors of their lives, but how can I spot people who already have these attributes when I'm hiring new staff members?

During the interview process, let potential employees know that each member of the company is expected to be a leader of his or her own job—and ask for the candidate's reaction. You may want to rule out anyone who is uncomfortable with this fact. A person who acts as a leader of his own life is by nature more energetic than one who follows others. Once you've hired a new employee, evaluate the employee mix in your department from time to time. This will help ensure that you don't have the right people in the wrong positions, which could prevent them from feeling like they can take the lead in their jobs.

—Yes, I believe in fighting against energy robbers, but how can I overcome my fear of taking risks—my biggest SOB?

There is no one answer for how to become more willing to take risks, but here are a few insights which might help. In one study on motivation, five-year-old children were given some rope rings and told to throw them on a peg without being told where to stand. The researchers found that the children who were failure-oriented stood either very close to or far away from the peg. Only those who were challenged by the possibility that they could succeed stood at a reasonable distance.

Secure people tend to take more risks. You may want to work on areas of your life that build security. One way is to choose friends and associates who will reaffirm and support you—but won't blindly endorse whatever you do. And don't forget that you're your own best friend. Set goals that are challenging, yet attainable. Then celebrate your accomplishments!

CHAPTER 5

Focusing Energy:
How to Get More Done
with Less Effort

I once read that it's possible to run a small stream of water with such force that it could cut through a piece of cake without leaving any crumbs. That type of concentrated energy reminds me of the highly directed light of lasers. Lasers are so focused and so manageable that they are used as surgical instruments to remove cataracts and skin pigmentation, and even to break up some "inoperable" tumors.

As a company leader, I've often wished I could focus my energy like a laser—to cut through the organizational morass, concentrate on the job at hand, and get more done in less time and with less effort. No matter how much energy my employees and I have, it's worthless unless it's harnessed, concentrated and used to its maximum advantage.

One of the ways we cut through the organizational layers at Pryor Resources, Inc., is by giving my administrative assistant the authority to go anywhere within the organization to make things happen and get what is needed from whoever has it. She is charged to move through the company like a laser to generate work and effect change.

But while my administrative assistant has this far-reaching authority, she knows that she can't bulldoze other employees into cooperating. She must be specific in communicating her purpose and goals so that employees understand exactly what she needs and why, and can better accommodate those needs.

"It's true that if I'm having trouble getting what I need, I can throw the weight of administration's name around. But I prefer to ask for myself, in a friendly yet assertive way," she says. "I don't waste time with flattery, but 'please' and 'thank you' go a long way to help me get what I'm after. Occasionally I've had to let colleagues know that getting my job done is more important than friendship. But if I'm firm and clear about my responsibilities, they are usually more than willing to help. I consider my job to be that of a public relations representative for administration. How I ask for things, and how efficiently things get done, directly reflects on management." Because of her ability to concentrate, my administrative assistant gets more done with less effort.

Her finely tuned sense of purpose and direction not only help other employees focus on the work they need to do, but insures that administration stays on track. In fact, our President, Phil Love, tells her that her biggest job is to keep us on an even keel—to show us when we've gone off on an inappropriate tangent, and when we have become inflexible or have blown an issue out of proportion.

In addition to giving employees the authority they need to focus their energy, we can also help relieve them of extraneous concerns and worries so they can approach a task single-mindedly. That may mean giving employees a sufficient amount of time to get the job done without the weight of an unrealistic deadline bogging them down. Or it may dictate that we have to learn to prioritize our needs so that not every task we assign is due at the same time—yesterday.

The next time you find yourself scattered all over the office with bits of your attention landing on various pieces of work, think back to how easy it was when you were a kid to become totally absorbed in a hobby or game. Growing up complicates our lives. The years seem to diffuse our ability to concentrate—just when we need it most.

By helping their staffs focus on a project, managers will allow employees to regain some of the fascination they had as children—and fascination leads to concentration. Because kids have fewer commitments and worries than adults, they live almost completely in the present and are rarely concerned about what happened yesterday or what tomorrow may bring. When a child eats an ice cream cone, he zeroes in on the taste of the treat, and 100 percent of his energy is focused on licking that cone. But because our attention is scattered over yesterday, today, and tomorrow, we adults can devour an entire cone without even tasting it—and in our preoccupation, we forfeit one more of life's pleasures.

When you allow for some of that kind of childlike concentration in your employees, you'll find they'll be with you in mind and spirit—not just in body. This gift of focusing helps people learn to see a task with fresh eyes and really understand what they're trying to do. It may also help them to find out if they've over-committed themselves. You can't be 100 percent committed to something if you are 5 percent committed to everything. Don't forget: you will influence employees more if, as their leader, you can model such focused behavior and be a living example of its benefits.

Have you been fascinated by anything recently? My wife and I were having dinner in a seafood restaurant in San Diego awhile back when a young couple walked in hand in hand, eyes riveted on each other. They sat down at a table near us and as soon as they were seated, they grabbed hands again. You could feel the electricity in their gaze. I looked over at Shirley and realized that we both had our hands firmly planted on the menu—we were only interested in *food*. When you've been married for 30 years, it's easy to get caught up in the blur of routine.

Learning to focus with greater intensity will also help you recapture a feeling of fascination with your job, making your experiences fuller, richer and more meaningful. Focusing on the job may mean taking a fresh and concentrated look at each of the five energy hot spots in your company, as outlined in Chapter 1—human resources, organizational structure, external markets, technology, and information systems. How do you spend money to attract external markets? As a manager, are you clear about what your cash flow really is? Have you overhired or underhired? Focusing means concentrating—siphoning energy away from the many other areas that are demanding your attention, and shining it like a spotlight on the one area you are interested in right now.

Focusing is a discipline that requires training and practice. It may be a tough task for individuals who eat the icing off the cake—those who require all the gratification of a job up front. But for those who are willing to do the work necessary to concentrate, focusing can be one of the launching points that enables them to rise above obstacles and become top performers.

Do Your Actions Reflect Your Values?

Have you noticed how you'll keep putting off a task like doing your taxes because you just can't seem to harness the time or the concentration? Yet you jump out of bed full of energy on Saturday morning to draw up plans for your new rec room. You focus more clearly and get your work done more quickly when you're excited about a project. You don't procrastinate or have trouble concentrating, because you anticipate the sense of achievement and fulfillment you'll feel when the work is complete. When you truly believe in *what* you're doing and *how* you're doing it, you are working toward clearly defined goals that stem from your values. Hard work and commitment naturally follow.

To learn to gather this same excitement for less pleasant tasks, try to create a clear mental picture of the end result. Focus on that, rather than the tedious or difficult steps leading to it, when you approach these tasks. Mentally place some sort of "carrot" lure in front of you, such as planning a mini-reward or celebration for getting closer to a goal.

Most of us have a very sharp image of what we want or need to get done. But often we're in such a hurry to get to the pot of gold at the end of the rainbow that we cash in our values along the way. Many people will tell you how wonderful their values are, but it's often just a song and dance. A good motto to observe is, "Don't listen to what they say, watch their feet." For instance, people may say they value their health, but they get so caught up in the work frenzy that they choke down fast food for breakfast, lunch, and dinner. And they'd probably see their running shoes more often if they had them bronzed and hung them above their desk. I know a public speaker who travels around the country and says things like, "My two children are the most important things in my life." Yet he's gone about 180 days a year. He's so busy providing *for* them that he doesn't give enough of himself *to* them. Listen to what you say you value, and make sure your actions are true to them.

One night I recall staring blankly at the television. I finally asked myself why I was sitting there and what I really valued. I decided the good feeling I'd have after presenting a well-prepared talk the next day was of more value to me than the program I was watching. Doing that made me focus on my real values, which gave me my goal (to get the speech written), established my priorities, and moved me toward what I wanted to achieve—a successful presentation.

Here's a simple illustration that shows the Achievement Loop we can follow in order to focus our energy and achieve our goals. Note how I got lassoed into writing my speech.

Achievement Loop	*"How to Write a Speech" Loop*
Values	A satisfied audience and the good feelings gained from presenting a well-prepared talk.
Goals	Finish writing the speech.
Priorities	The speech is more important than the television sitcom.
Conviction	Being prepared is essential.
Action	I turned off the TV and went upstairs to the study.
Results	A completed speech.
ACHIEVEMENT	Applause from a satisfied audience.
	(Note the similarity between this and the values with which the loop started!)

Rethinking our values will keep us from waking up one morning and suddenly realizing that we're not achieving the way other people are—perhaps realizing that we have met some of our goals, but only at the expense of other things that we truly valued.

Do you let your goals overshadow your values? For instance, you may say you value being on the cutting edge of technology, yet you become so concerned with meeting production goals that you don't give employees opportunities to be creative and innovative. Or you may say you value good employee relationships, but the pressure to get things done always seems more important than allocating time for employees to attend seminars or participate in wellness programs.

Many corporate executives are realizing that people work most effectively and energetically when they share common values with their managers and their organizations, and believe that the work they do has meaning and purpose. One way to help employees understand your values and focus their energy is through a technique called "framing." Instead of handing staff members assignments cold, give them an entire framework within which to view the task and warm up to it. That means making sure they understand:

—Exactly what you want them to do;

—How their work relates to the goals of the company;

—The values underlying those goals;

—The assumptions people in the organization are making about the situation;

—The fears and hopes connected with it;

—The costs that may be incurred; and

—The authority you are giving the employees.

As managers, our tendency is to be task-oriented toward our employees and not involve them in the overall plan for the department and company. We may say, "Steve, I want you to take this new budgeting process and put it into place." If that's all the information we share, Steve doesn't understand some of the key components of the new system; he doesn't know anything about your preconceived ideas about how it should be implemented, and what expectations top management has for its unqualified success.

Even though we may encourage employees to be *directors* of their own lives and jobs, that doesn't mean they don't need *direction* from management. Larry Wheeler, of Marion Laboratories, says that management at his company holds itself responsible for providing clarity in three specific areas. "We must provide clarity of *direction* so that we are all headed toward the same goal, clarity of *structure*, so that we know whose job it is to do what, and clarity of *measurement* so that we know how we are going to measure whether or not we meet our goals," he says. "If management does a good job in those areas, then the smartest thing we can do is get out of the way— because we've got the people who can get the job done and who can do it better than anyone else."

In Chapter 1, I talked about Dick Slember, Ph.D., general manager of the Nuclear Fuels Division of Westinghouse, and how he posts the business unit's goals on mission statements and graphs that are hung on the wall just outside his office for all employees to see. To further help his staff focus on the "pulse points" that are critical to the success of his organization, Slember holds monthly teleconferencing meetings so that managers and supervisors at all three of the organization's sites can take part. Sitting in a conference room and linked electronically to his staff, Slember takes two hours to review 140 specific quality and production measurements.

"When we first implemented this system, I'd ask my supervisors what they planned to do to improve a particular pulse point measure. They would frequently provide fuzzy answers, primarily because their management attention had not been focused on the trends in question," says Slember. "Thus, what should have been a two hour process took forever. But today everyone knows exactly what measurements we are going to look at. They understand the process—identify, focus attention, and act!

"If the numbers aren't where they should be, our line managers know it, often before I do, and they will take actions to correct the situation without waiting for a meeting to review the issue. The process is simple. We look at a problem, we trend it, and we post it. Once we spotlight a problem, we know our people will find ways to improve it. They know that if it weren't important to me and the company, we wouldn't make a chart out of it and put it on the wall or expect to talk about it during the conference. Employees want to see improvement and want to do a good job. But you can't expect either of those results unless you get everyone to share the same vision and the same values, and get everyone—management and employees—singing from the same song sheet."

When employees understand the entire picture, it's easier for them to feel excited about their work and to have a greater sense of commitment to it. Having conviction about a job—rather than just going through the motions—will help them set priorities and do their best. And when they successfully complete a job, they'll feel energized and want to succeed again. The cycle keeps itself in motion.

Asking Just One Question Will Help Keep Priorities in Check

If I offered you a choice of cash gifts of $100, $20, or $10, which would you choose? You'd probably choose the $100 without hesitation. That choice seems obvious, but when we try to manage our time, we often do the less important $10 items when we should start with the more-important $100 tasks.

Take a few minutes to analyze your workday. Do you find yourself reading insignificant material or answering unimportant phone calls when you should be tackling a project you've been putting off for weeks? Do you ever go home knowing that, although every minute of your day was filled, you accomplished little of what you wanted to achieve?

Unfinished work creates tremendous stress and anxiety because it makes us feel vulnerable and out of control. And since experts in stress management have told me that people who don't manage stress well often die as much as 15 years before they should, learning how to get things done can literally add years to your life.

One way to keep your priorities in focus is to ask yourself continually, "Is this the most important thing I could be doing right now?" If you can answer "yes," then chances are you're living by your priorities. If not, you may be letting circumstances control your time.

A daily "To Do" list will help you do things according to priority. Number the items on the list in order of importance and check them off as you complete them. If you do things that aren't on your list, write down those items and check them off as well. Then instead of wondering where your time went, you'll be able to see the many things you accomplished and focus on your achievements rather than on what didn't get done. At the end of the day, when you transfer the items you didn't do to the next day's list, you'll be able to judge whether you've done things according to priority.

A To Do list will also help you explain your priorities to others. If your boss asks you to do something that will affect another project's timing, you can pull out your list and say, "I'm willing to put in the additional hours of work, but which of these items would you like me to postpone so that I can do what you've just given me?"

That kind of feedback is effective because it is specific and backed up with information that justifies your position. It's much more effective than simply complaining that you don't have time, which doesn't offer any explanation for why that new project shouldn't be of highest priority.

Three Tips for Earning Big Returns on Time Investments

Just as you invest your money in ways that will get the best possible yield, it's important to get the best "Return On Time Investments" (ROTI).

In most organizations, meetings are one of the biggest time-wasters. Most meetings include too many people and take too much of their time. Have you attended a two-hour meeting when you only needed to be there for 20 minutes? Have you ever been at a meeting with a number of other managers— whose salaries for the hour-long meeting totaled hundreds of dollars—to discuss a $100 item? If you performed a cost analysis on those types of meetings, you'd see that they have horrendous ROTI factors.

One of the ways to make meetings productive is to stop and ask people what is on their mind. Maybe someone in the group is fantasizing about the fish and fries he plans to order for lunch instead of focusing on the budget. Or someone else might still be mulling over a point made minutes earlier because he doesn't fully understand it but is afraid to break in and say so. Employees need to feel free to talk about what is on their minds.

Their input will help you realize when energy levels are low or if certain points warrant better explanations. You'll find that taking this quick refocusing break will help bring everyone else back from their daydreams and into the heart of the meeting.

Another way we get a poor return on our time investment is by hiring someone new and putting off fully training that person because we think we don't have the time. Instead, higher-paid staff members continue to do work that could be delegated to the new employee—a poor ROTI.

Finally, evaluate your ROTI by employing Pareto's Law. Pareto was the famous Italian economist mentioned in Chapter 2, who determined that, frequently, 20 percent of an effort put forth yields 80 percent of the result. With that in mind, you might determine how you can use your unproductive time more effectively and beat Pareto's Law. If 20 percent of the meetings your department holds is getting 80 percent of the work done, many of the meetings are probably unnecessary. And if 20 percent of your staff is doing the majority of the work, maybe it's time to make some changes to increase the energy levels and productivity of the remaining 80 percent.

Organize Today—Because You Won't Have Time to Redo Things Tomorrow

Another way to get the best possible ROTI is to look at how you organize your work. But before you embark on a new organizational system, make sure it will work for you. People with messy desks often can find what they need when they need it and can do an extraordinary job. But if you waste time looking for important papers or rewriting lost reports, chances are it's time to reorganize.

One simple way to divide and conquer your work is to use colored folders in your filing system. Use a red folder for items that must be dealt with immediately, a blue folder for the next most pressing tasks, and a yellow folder for tasks with less urgent deadlines. Set aside a specific time of day to review the contents of each folder.

When you go through the folders, other paperwork, and

mail, try to be as efficient as possible and handle each piece of paper only once. To see how well you're doing, use the "chicken pox approach." Each time you pick up a piece of paper, put a red dot in the right-hand corner. You may be surprised to see that, by the time you finally take action, the paper has got a case of chicken pox!

Instead of shuffling paper, deal immediately with each piece. As soon as you read a letter, dictate a reply for your secretary to type, or, if appropriate, write a response on the bottom of the correspondence. Instead of burying a question-naire in the bottom of your in-basket, answer it immediately or toss it out. Don't save memos that list only the time and date of a meeting. Instead, transfer that information to your calendar and toss the memo in the wastebasket. If a memo includes a detailed agenda, put the date on your calendar and place the memo into the file for the relevant project.

Perfectionists often find it difficult to take immediate action. Instead of concentrating on the job in the amount of time available, they put off doing it, thinking that they'll have more time later to do a more thorough job. But by the time they get to the project, they are often forced to work under deadline pressure. They waste time and energy trying to track down people and information; whereas, if they had done it earlier, they could have scheduled meetings and had others help them gather the necessary data.

Don't get caught up in the tyranny of the urgent. Using your time to put out brush fires doesn't help you work effec-tively or efficiently. When you have to blaze through something, you often don't produce quality work. Next time you think you don't have the time to concentrate on a project, ask yourself this question: "If I don't have time to do things right today, when will I have the time to do them over?"

Scheduling Your Day Around Energy Peaks and Valleys

When babies are tired and hungry, they cry; when adults are tired and hungry, they get irritable. While we wouldn't think of ignoring a baby when it cries, we persistently schedule meetings or pick times to work on important projects at times when people are tired and hungry and have the least amount of concentration.

If you work often enough with someone, you know if he is a "morning" or "afternoon" person. But even if you don't know someone's workstyle, there are certain time metabolism principles that hold true for most individuals.

In a regular eight-hour workday, most people are geared up from the time they get to work until hunger sets in—usually around 11 a.m. From lunchtime until about 1:30 p.m. when their food is digested, people often feel sleepy and lethargic. Then from 1:30 p.m. to about 4:30 p.m., their energy levels increase again.

Whenever possible, avoid scheduling meetings or talking about important issues just before lunch, when people's stomachs and mouths are growling, or during the late afternoon, when their tempers and attention spans are short.

Paying attention to time metabolism will help you make the most efficient use of your time. If you are most energetic in the morning, tackle the most difficult projects then. It might be a good time of day for you to schedule meetings that require a lot of interaction and brainstorming. Reserve the afternoon, when you have less energy, for more routine tasks like returning phone calls and filling out reports.

Take a break when you're feeling tired and, preferably, after every 45 minutes of concentrated work. Stand up and stretch, take a brisk walk, or close your eyes for a minute or two to send your mind on a vacation. You'll find that taking time to pause will help you gain a new perspective. While your body is doing something different, your subconscious may be working out solutions to the problem. Or while you're away, you may realize that the issue wasn't as important as it seemed at the time.

Learning to Say "No" to Prevent Interruptions

Whether it's answering a phone call that breaks your concentration, or stopping to talk to an employee and arriving late for a meeting, interruptions can be one of the biggest problems you face in managing time and work. And if you give in to every interruption, you'll waste valuable time, dissipate your energy, and be frustrated by your lack of achievement.

Preventing interruptions sometimes means learning to say "no." If you're working on a deadline and someone asks to talk to you, you may have to tell them that you don't have time now, but they can make an appointment to talk with you later. If you agree to speak with them briefly, keep an eye on your watch and make sure you keep the meeting short.

To keep your mind on a project, replace your "open-door" policy with a "screen-door policy" that will help you determine whether an interruption is urgent, semi-urgent, or something that can wait until you have more time. Ask your secretary to use her judgment and to interrupt you only when necessary. Or if you don't have a secretary, try mounting three vertical files marked "Urgent," "Semi-Urgent", and "Can Wait" on your office door. Ask co-workers to drop a note in the appropriate file rather than interrupting you. You can see which file they drop the note into and then judge when you will need to get back to them. Or, check the files whenever you take a break.

Sometimes your own staff may demand so much time that you may wonder if you'd be better off doing everything yourself. Help your employees become independent by asking that before they bring problems to your attention, they write down the problem and three possible solutions, as well as deciding on the best of the three.

While going through that process, employees will probably decide on the best solution themselves. They'll realize that they don't need your assistance, or that they only need to ask for your approval on their decision. At the very least they will organize their thoughts, and your meeting with them will be shorter and more productive. They will have grown in the process, as well.

Are Telephone Calls Putting a Hold on Your Day?

Answering telephone calls not only takes up time but disrupts your concentration. It's essential to teach the person who answers your phone how to screen calls and determine which calls need to be answered immediately and which calls you can return later. But remember that telephone tag is a time-waster: you can spend more time returning calls from hard-to-get people than you would if you had talked to them when they first called.

Whenever possible, group your return calls together and try to make them at a time when you will need a break from more intense work. Before you place an important call, make a list of items you want to discuss. Then, during the conversation, take notes to help you to remember the main points once you've hung up.

A three-minute timer can help you keep calls as short as possible. Turn the timer over when the conversation starts and hold yourself accountable to the deadline. As the sand begins to run out, wind up the conversation.

Ending a conversation so that you can get back to other work is better than being preoccupied while you're on the phone. People can sense if you're not giving them your full attention. They'll recognize the lack of interest in your voice or a lack of continuity in your response.

There are polite cues that you can give to let the caller know you need to end the conversation. Thank the person for calling or summarize the discussion, which gives him the assurance that you understand what he said. But don't alienate people by being too abrupt. And even though you may think that you are being pleasant and accommodating, you may be coming across as insensitive and intolerant. (To discover how you sound to others, tape-record your side of a few conversations and evaluate your conversation skills or ask for feedback from others.)

The Delegation Factor: It Will Multiply Your Efforts

In addition to asking yourself, "Is this the most important thing I could be doing right now?" also ask yourself, "Could I delegate this work to someone else?"

Delegating work is one of the most powerful tools you can use to get more done. But if you're like most people, you won't assign as much work as you should. People are reluctant to delegate work for which they will be responsible, because they don't trust their ability to choose the right person for the job, don't trust the other person's ability to do the work, or simply don't realize that, to accomplish more, they have to stop trying to do everything themselves.

It's natural to want to do things the way we've always done them. The Peter Principle states that people tend to rise to their level of incompetence. I don't think it happens just because people are incompetent; I think it's because they lack confidence in their ability to be successful at the new job. Instead of recognizing that their new jobs call for a different set of priorities and skills and a new attitude, they continue to function as they did in their previous positions.

To be as effective as possible, it's essential not to involve ourselves in jobs that others can do for us. Take the necessary time to teach those who work for you how to do the job in a way that is acceptable to you.

But since everyone does things differently, don't expect that the work you delegate will be done exactly as you would have done it. Acknowledge other people's strengths and encourage them to be innovative. You'll discover great resources and loyalties in people whom you help to grow financially, personally, and professionally.

The most common definition of management is "getting things done through others." But people resent feeling that they're being used and knowing that they won't be recognized for their work. Effective management means getting things done through other people *while helping them grow in the process.* By investing in others, you invest in yourself. You multiply your energies and efforts and, in turn, get more done.

Yes, but . . .

So, you want to play devil's advocate, just to see if I really believe what I've said. In fact, you've probably been saying to yourself:

—Yes, Fred, it all sounds good, but I have so much to do that it often seems faster to do things myself than to delegate to employees.

That's an issue President Harry Truman eventually had to wrestle with. A story is told of a time when he was a senator and his secretary was at lunch and someone came into his office and asked him for a certain document. Rather than telling the person that his secretary would find the document when she returned, he spent 30 minutes of his time looking for it. Months later he became President and had to shift into high gear, and could no longer waste time performing tasks someone else could as easily do. Suddenly, learning to delegate and how to say "no" became extremely important.

—Yes, I've used the colored folder filing system and organizer notebooks, but none of those gimmicks seem to work for long.

No matter what daily planning system you use, it's the concept of prioritizing activities that's important. Our natural tendency is to react to what appears to be the most urgent event, to what captures our attention. For example, we subconsciously avoid working on a project that's due by returning a less-urgent phone call instead. But this haphazard approach is infinitely more costly in time and effort than it would be to list projects and then order them according to importance.

Most important: do tasks in their order of importance. By following a plan, you will experience fewer crises and get better results.

CHAPTER 6

Discovering the Power
of Positive Management:
Tune in to Trust
and Receive Cooperation

Three men who'd been marooned on an island for years dreamed that someday they'd be able to go home. One day while they were fishing, a bottle washed up on shore. A genie popped out and said, "I grant you each one wish."

"I know what I want," the first one said, "I want to go home." His wish was granted—and poof!—he was home. "I want to go home, too," the second fellow said, and up he went in a cloud of smoke.

The third guy thought awhile and said, "I want to make sure I know exactly what I want, so I'll take a few days to think about it." He reflected and mused, "You know these have been tough years, but pretty good ones, too. John and Jim were super guys—sure do miss them. I wish they were here . . ."

Sometimes you and I don't realize how much influence other people have on our lives. Nor are we aware of the cooperative spirit it takes to get things done to everyone's satisfaction.

The network of people behind your company's profit and loss statement must somehow work together to keep the organization running in the black. These employees are not paid to get along with each other. But the ones who do make an effort to meet the needs of others discover that in turn, their own needs get met. In short, we can't win if we're defeating others along the way. Even the shark—the ogre of the ocean—can sink his teeth into the win/win philosophy.

Sharks reputedly have indiscriminate palates and will dine on almost any ocean dweller—except the pilot fish. Instead, they invite the pilot fish over *after* lunch; then, the smaller fish acts as nature's toothpick, eating the leftover food lodged between the shark's teeth. It's a symbiotic relationship: the shark gets clean teeth and the pilot fish gets a full stomach. In other words, each fish gets its needs met.

The remarkable relationship between these two fish is possible for two reasons. First, the pilot fish trusts the shark not to eat it. Second, each fish knows that if it cooperates, it will ultimately benefit.

Trust and cooperation are essential to the success of any ecosystem—be it the depths of the ocean or the heights of the organizational structure. One of the surest ways to build trust among the people you work with is to be authentic. That means being spontaneous, not contrived; open and honest, not judgmental. It means working to avoid patronizing or condescending remarks, and it means displaying an attitude of "I only succeed when you succeed," and "Let's worry about *what* the problem is, not *who* the problem is."

The ability to be authentic, or to display other positive personality traits—patience, understanding, enthusiasm—that help us work with others, won't eliminate conflicts on the job. But they *will* help us deal with problems in a more constructive and expedient manner.

Managers who are inconsistent, or lack integrity with employees, pay the price. If I act one way toward certain employees and a different way toward others, my staff may question my integrity and lose trust in me. But if I create a climate of consistency, openness, and honesty, employees won't feel that they always have to be looking over their shoulders and wondering what I'm *really* thinking about them.

The surest way to develop authenticity is to think in terms of lifestyle, not leadership style. One of the nicest things that's happened in business in recent years is that people are realizing that they perform best if they take a holistic approach. That means being a total person—not being Jekyll at work and Hyde at home. How we act at home directly influences our behavior at the office. If we're working to become an effective individual at the office, we're also practicing becoming an extraordinary spouse, parent, and friend—and vice versa.

If we can learn to tell the people we live with that we love them, we're more likely to be able to express appreciation for people at work. Often it may seem that patting employees on the back is a frivolous waste of time. After all, isn't the pay we give our staff enough? Must we pay them compliments as well? Besides, if we haven't fired them, our employees ought to know we appreciate them.

Is this a familiar scenario? Your husband or wife complains, "You never tell me you love me anymore." You take your cue and mumble, "Of course I love you." But inside you're thinking, "Silly, I wouldn't be living with you if I didn't love you. But if that status changes, you'll be among the first to know."

Some of us are so doggedly self-driven that we act as if we don't need anybody. My wife occasionally accuses me of that. She says, "Fred, you probably wouldn't even show up at my funeral—you'd be out dating." And I insist, "Shirley, that's not true. *We'd* be there." Sometimes I act as if I don't need Shirley, but the truth is I do. It's just that I don't tell her all the time, because I think she's supposed to read between the lines.

It's easy to act aloof or indifferent toward the people we work with, too. We're so busy talking to people who *aren't* doing a good job that we don't take the time to recognize the people who *are* performing well. When that happens, we managers can't understand how the people we really count on—those apples of our eye—could turn rotten.

Just as children learn to get attention any way they can—even by misbehaving—some adults learn that the only way to get attention is to do something wrong. When Joe arrives at work late, we take note and say, "Joe, you're late."

Joe thinks to himself, "Gee, that's the first time you've spoken to me in weeks." So Joe starts showing up late all the time and tells his friend, "Now that I'm coming in late, everybody notices me—in fact they're having meetings about me."

People thrive on attention, and it's much smarter to give them positive attention than negative, because our actions often determine and reinforce behavior in others. Sometimes our employees with the healthiest attitudes are the ones who need to be nourished the most. We need to recognize the people who are our assets rather than dwell on those who are liabilities.

Do you tell your employees when they do things well? Do you compliment them on the way they handled a tough client? The degree to which we give people what they need is the degree to which they'll give us what we need to run a successful operation. An institute in Chicago reported that a manager's success can be attributed 15 percent to technical skills and 85 percent to human relations skills. It's so simple and so powerful, yet so few people really work at perfecting those skills.

Management from the Bottom Up: Supporting Staff with Resources and Opportunities

I don't know what your introduction into the business arena was like, but many of us were indoctrinated into a fear-oriented environment. The classical image of a manager was someone who tried to control people—an autocrat who distanced himself from employees. He may have said something like, "Joanne, I'm very glad you came on board. I think you should be proud of the fact that you were selected from a field of 25 candidates—and, incidentally, we held onto the other 24 names."

That strong-arm style of management worked in the past because the manager controlled the workforce, and the workforce controlled the equipment. That's not a bad arrangement because equipment needs to be controlled—it has to be oiled, tuned, and cleaned on a regular basis to work most efficiently.

But our culture shifted and today the majority of our workforce is involved in the service industry. So, if I'm a controlling manager, you'll follow my lead: the way you interface with customers will reflect the way I treat you. When a client says, "I'd like some help," you say, "Well, what do you want?" or "Don't complain to me. I've got enough problems of my own handling customer relations."

The big problem with working under the premise that management is getting things done through others, is that employees feel short-changed. But if I get things done through my employees while building them in the process, they get more than a paycheck in return for their efforts. They come away feeling good about themselves, their manager, and the company.

Building people means letting them learn to do their job, not telling them how to do it. Many managers are hands-on leaders who like to show employees exactly what to do and how to do it, and don't afford employees the opportunity to determine creatively how they can perform best.

A dictatorial manager tries to control employees' time, energy, conversations, and work environment. He sees it as his responsibility to stay on top of employees, always wanting to know what they're doing and when they're doing it. He wants hourly reports, thinking he must keep close watch to prevent employees from doing something stupid. This watchdog approach makes people feel like animals.

The truth is, the person who does the job day in and day out probably has the best perspective about how that job needs to be done. And even if figuring out how to do the job is harder than having someone else clue him in, the employee will have more energy and commitment because he'll have a sense of involvement and participation.

Invest in People—Don't Use Them

One of the best ways to keep positive energies flowing among the people we manage is to create an environment that lets employees direct their own activities and feel responsible for the outcome of their work. This technique, called "resourcing," requires that we give employees the resources they need—support, time or budget—to do their jobs. Management's primary responsibility is to match job requirements with the available resources to get it done, and a manager's role is to be an *investor in* people rather than a *user of* people.

In this sense, the responsibility for a product or service is shared by everyone within the company. We move away from the mentality of the production-line worker who says, "They really have a stupid system here, but I'm not responsible," to someone who says, "I can see a better way to do this and I want to share my ideas with management." This is not to say that management should abdicate all its responsibilities and authority to employees, but to suggest that managers invite employees to help them find ways to work most effectively.

That may mean turning your current organizational chart upside down. A company that resources its employees operates with an inverted pyramid-style organizational chart with management on the bottom, supporting employees.

If the idea of resourcing conjures up images of management bowing to employees, let me explain what resourcing is *not*. Resourcing is not giving the store away. It's not giving an inch and having employees take a mile. It's not making a sensitivity group out of your company. And it's not taking a vote on every decision.

A resourcing manager does not have to endorse everything an employee does or cater to his or her every whim. But a manager should at least be fair and take the employee's point of view into consideration before making a decision. Finally, resourcing does not mean that you do your employees' work; it means you set up expectations—you let them know that you expect them to have goals and to take charge of their jobs.

I believe the most efficient and effective type of manager is one who knows how to manage resources as well as people. We've all heard stories about the high-paid professionals who complain that they are wasting time photocopying, answering the phone, and performing other clerical tasks. When they suggest that a clerk be hired to do these things, the boss tells them that when profits increase, he'll spend the money to hire extra help.

Could you imagine a coach telling his players that they will have to clean up the locker room after the games until they start winning more? Instead, he provides his players with the time, equipment, and training they need to play the best they can. The players' job is to give winning the old college try. As managers, we coach people to be successful. In return we expect them to carry the ball.

Cutting the Cord: How to Avoid Employee Dependency

A management consultant was called in to analyze the management team of a large computer company. Seven years ago the company began a management training program. The president, whom I'll call Tony, hand-picked the people for the program, enrolled them, led them, and rewarded them upon completion. He thought he would launch a strong crew of leaders with the "right stuff," but he wound up with a weak flock of followers because he had done everything for them, never encouraging them to test their wings.

The consultant went to Tony's house to discuss the situation and quickly noticed how Tony and his wife interacted with their two-year-old son. When the toddler finished his milk, they leaped up to get him more. When the youngster cried when he didn't get his way, both parents tried to pacify him with toys and treats. In other words, Ivan the terrible two-year-old ruled the house. The consultant realized that Tony coddled his employees the same way he did his son. By doing everything for his managers, Tony had created an organization full of two-year-olds.

Tony changed his management style and told his people that he would help them become good managers but would not sign them up for courses any longer. He told them he expected them to be self-initiating and competent, and that he would no longer stand for passive employees.

Unlike the controlling manager who tells employees what to do and how to do it, the resourcing manager invests in people and expects something in return. This type of manager is not patriarchal with employees because, just as teenagers resent being dependent on parents, employees resent having to depend on their boss.

One of the best ways I know to avoid making people dependent on us is to include them in the decisions affecting what they will be held accountable for. If you do that, you'll probably find that your employees may be harder on themselves than you would have been.

You might say, "How are we going to know if this department is successful? And one year from now, what will we have accomplished?" Those kinds of questions help employees commit themselves to goals. And then if you ask, "What do we have to do to make things happen? And what are your responsibilities?" they begin to formulate action plans to meet those goals.

Are You Making Yourself Look Good at Others' Expense?

Managers sometimes abuse the process of delegation—they give employees tasks but keep them dependent by not giving them all the information they need. That happens when a manager believes that the only way he can feel good about himself is if others can't function without him.

We all have a desire to feel important, but as psychologist

Abraham Maslow wrote in his book *Toward a Psychology of Being*, (2nd edition, Van Nostrand Reinhold Company, 1968), that desire becomes a deficiency need when we get our needs met at other people's expense. If, as your manager, I keep you dependent on me, you will begin to sense that I'm using you to bolster my self-image. And if you come up with a good idea and I go to a department managers' meeting and present your idea as mine, you'll probably find out about it, see my lack of integrity, and lose respect for me. It's a lose/lose situation. In trying to arm myself with respect and self-confidence, I've shot myself in the foot.

The best thing I can do when you come up with a great idea is say, "I was talking with Victoria a few minutes ago, and she came up with a super idea. And that's something she does consistently." That doesn't make me look bad; in fact, the people at the meeting will say, "You know, that Fred Pryor really builds people. Isn't that nice he acknowledged Victoria instead of trying to take the credit for her idea. I bet Victoria really likes working with Fred."

GIVE THE EMPLOYEE THE CREDIT.

Building Self-Esteem Through a Strong Support Network

It may be time to honestly evaluate how we, as managers, get our needs met. If we seem to be operating out of desperation for attention and recognition, we should look for other ways to feel good about ourselves that don't involve diminishing others. We can do that by establishing supportive relationships with others. Good friends can be one of your primary assets. They don't like you just because you're smart or talented; they like you for *you.*

But building friendships is not easy; it means we have to reach out and take risks. What if I said I liked you and you said, "Yuck!?" It's difficult to take risks, but if you want to establish good relationships you have to start trusting yourself and others.

A good way to learn to trust is through self-disclosure. For example, I might say, "Roger, I'm frustrated because there seems to be tension between us, and I'd sure like to know what I can do to change that."

Risking that type of statement may generate valuable feedback and be the beginning of a trusting relationship. But I have to be careful that I don't wear you thin. Instead of clinging to one person, I have to work on establishing relationships with others as well. I can do that by offering to help someone else instead of waiting for someone to help me. I can compliment others and ask someone I admire out to lunch. If you set some goals that are reasonable you'll accomplish them and begin to see that others will accept and like you.

11 Attributes of a Resourcing Manager

The old-style manager plays benevolent dictator—*allowing* people to earn good salaries, and letting them receive praise only when he feels good about himself—but the resourcing manager *provides opportunities* for employees to excel and be recognized.

Take a minute to look at the difference between the controlling and resourcing manager:

The Controlling Manager fosters . . .	The Resourcing Manager fosters . . .
Dependency	Independence
Obligation	Freedom
Hopelessness	Hope
Pessimism	Optimism
Suspicion	Trust
Time-clock mentality	Excitement
Exhaustion	Energy
Stinginess of spirit	Generosity
Regulations	Objectives
Secrecy	Openness
Guilt	Fulfillment

Now compare how the employee feels who works for these two different types of managers:

The Controlled Employee feels . . .	*The Resourced Employee feels . . .*
Passive	Energized
Angry	Happy
Uninformed	Involved
Diminished	Respected
Hostile	Amiable

All this boils down to the simple fact that the energetic manager treats employees as well as he treats himself. He acts as a role model or mentor who shows the way, encourages, and advocates. If as a leader you set an excellent example, employees catch the spirit of your example. That's where we get the saying, "Leadership is much more caught than taught." For example, if a manager listens with great attention, his actions let his employees know that he values their input, rather than discounting the employee with mannerisms that say, "I don't have time for you."

The energetic type of manager operates under the premise that his employees make a difference. It matters to him whether an employee is upbeat or dispirited, angry or accepting. To be an effective manager, we have to avoid the mentality that says, "This is my company (or my department) and I'm going to *allow* this to happen." Our businesses will blossom when employees work with an entrepreneurial attitude that says, "This is our company."

I have heard that John D. Rockefeller used to make the following claim: "If you took all my money away and left my people, I'd build my wealth again." I feel that if we believe in and live by this philosophy, that people are what make a company, we can make a significant difference in our organization's bottom line.

How Leadership Style Influences
Commitment and Intensity

Most of us find it easier and more rewarding to work with people who are content in their jobs. And the employees who are most dedicated and satisfied are the ones who know that management is pulling for them. When they feel they're a vital part of the team, they become highly committed to the organization's goals and advance toward them with intensity.

Here's a simple chart that illustrates how the relationship between commitment and intensity affects performance:

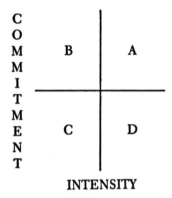

C
O
M   B   A
M
I
T
M
E   C   D
N
T

INTENSITY

A: High intensity, high commitment
= getting somewhere...fast

B: High commitment, low intensity
= getting somewhere...slowly

C: Low intensity, low commitment
= getting nowhere...slowly

D. Low commitment, high intensity
= getting nowhere...fast

The way we treat those we work with directly influences their levels of commitment and intensity. If we are overly critical of our employees, their energies are misspent fighting bad feelings. They—and in turn the organization—go nowhere . . . fast.

To keep intensity and commitment high, we need to encourage others and let them know that we're interested in and concerned about them. This way we all get where we want to go . . . fast!

One essential—yet often overlooked—element in working with people is understanding the need for rejuvenation. Managers who understand the correlation between rejuvenation and productivity encourage employees to take their lunch breaks, knock off at a reasonable time, and use their vacation to get away from the office rather than taking the hours in pay.

Those same managers are alert to behavior that indicates that an employee is suffering from a draining personal problem. They notice rapid weight gain, strained relationships at work, chronic illness, alcohol or drug abuse, an inability to concentrate, and temperamental or defensive behavior. But, instead of telling employees to leave their problems at home, supportive managers help their people confront and overcome problems. They know that troubles on the home front can easily affect the job employees do at work. And while they try to help employees work these troubles out, intuitive managers also recognize when the problem has grown beyond their capabilities and when professional attention is warranted.

A Different Kind of PERK That Makes Employees Respond with VIGOR

Adopting a holistic approach toward management, one that shows concern for employees as individuals, not just a nameless work force, is a healthy and profitable way to do business. Today, more and more company leaders are managing holistically—not out of benevolence but out of necessity. It's become strikingly clear that it's the dedication of people, not the intimidation of them, that gets things done.

One way to build loyalty is by showing employees that you appreciate their work. How? It's true that employees appreciate extra benefits management gives to recognize a job well done—bonuses, awards, and "Employee of the Month" parking spaces—but people don't like to be bought. I believe that there is a different kind of PERK that is infinitely more powerful and leaves employees with a greater sense of dignity and pride. This kind of PERK puts us in charge as directors of our lives—it's the kind that's spelled:

> **P—Participation.** As a manager, do you independently make decisions that influence others and then tell employees that

what you've decided will make them happy? Managers who act that way deprive people of a sense of involvement. People who get a chance to participate in their destiny feel energized. I suggest that you seriously look at giving people in your company an opportunity to take an active role in decisions that affect the organization's values, goals and direction. It may not be an easy task, but it's a whole lot easier than solving the problems that can result if you don't give them the chance.

E—Expectations. Do you know someone who strongly believes in you? If so, you know how great that feels. When you have a positive sense of expectation about someone, you empower him and increase the effectiveness of your relationship. Having expectations also means letting others know what you want. When you tell employees what you expect, they're more likely to produce what you want. And if you let people know that you expect them to succeed, they are more likely to do so.

R—Recognition—not only in the form of awards and pay increases, but recognition on a regular basis that comes from praise, compliments, and encouragement. Letting employees know that you are interested in them and aware of the contributions they make helps build their sense of pride and commitment.

K—Know-how. It's teaching them. Communicating with them. Helping them to learn and grow. Many managers don't care what anyone else knows and never take the time to tell employees what is going on. They are so busy they assume their staff knows what is happening, but in reality the staff feels uninformed. If we want to resource people, we've got to help them know as much or more than we do.

S—Satisfaction. Employees feel best when they are the directors of their own jobs and not dependent on management. Try letting employees set their own goals about performance levels. You'll see that when they achieve objectives they set for themselves, they will gain a great sense of pride. When you have a group of satisfied people, you can't help but have a nice place to work.

When you give employees that kind of PERK they respond with a sense of VIGOR:

V—Vitality results when employees receive recognition. They perform their jobs with enthusiasm and excitement.

I—Interest. When employees feel appreciated, their interest in their work and the company increases.

G—Goal-Orientation—the mind-set employees have when they are included in the company's vision.

O—Ownership employees feel when they are encouraged to become *"intrapreneurs"*—entrepreneurs within the organization. These employees are free to create, innovate, and dream. They take ownership in what they do and know that their input makes a difference.

R—Responsibility the energetic leader wants his employees to have about their work.

When employees feel that management cares about their contributions, they feel a sense of ownership in the company and are eager to give more of themselves. Success, in any organization, hinges on the ability to help people achieve their goals and to keep them challenged. When you fuel people's interest in the company by providing new growth opportunities, you will ignite the spirit they had when they were hired. And when you spark that kind of excitement, job satisfaction is a natural result.

Yes, but . . .

Yes, all this talk about resourcing sounds good, but I live by the philosophy "If it ain't broke don't fix it." Some say I am closed-minded, but why should I change my tactics if my department is running smoothly?

It may be easier to accept the possibility that you could be somewhat closed-minded if you see how common it is. When Marchese Guglielmo Marconi told his friends that he had discovered a way to send messages through the air without wires, they promptly committed him to a psychiatric ward. And when a young salesman was asked by the Hookless Fastener Company how they could increase the sales of their zippers, the man came up with the idea of using them instead of buttons on the front of men's pants. No one believed the idea would fly. But years later the company, now Talon Manufacturing, realized the worth of the idea they almost turned down.

Too often we live inside our own heads and have a biased point of view. Before you bar the door to your mind, remember that just because your operating mode is working doesn't mean another approach may not be better for *you* and your employees.

—Yes, I know it's important to provide training and development opportunities for employees. But it seems that whenever I invest a lot in an employee, the person leaves for a higher-paying job.

It's a fact of life that there's nothing you can do to keep some people. That doesn't mean we should stop offering them opportunities to grow. In fact, there's no better, more cost-effective investment we can make than to enhance the skills and knowledge of our work force. We only win when our people win.

CHAPTER 7

Transmitting Energy:
Are Your Communication Lines
Clear Enough to Hear a Pin Drop?

What kind of communication lines run through your organization? Are they exposed, high-voltage wires that jolt anyone who dares to voice opinions that differ from management's? Are they dead or short-circuited, disconnecting management from the needs of the work force and clients? Or are your lines of communication properly routed and insulated, giving people the power to say what's on their minds without jeopardizing their reputations or their jobs?

Of all the training-program requests made to Pryor Resources, Inc., requests for programs to enhance communication skills rank at the top. In fact, surveys of seminar attendees we conducted singled out lack of communication between bosses and workers as the biggest problem in the workplace.

To me, there is no interpersonal skill more important than being able to communicate your wants and needs to those you work with, while letting them know that you care about their

115

individual needs. Employers and employees alike must talk and listen to each other, because to allow energy to move through an organization, we have to facilitate its transit. When we open our minds and our lines of communication, it's a lot easier for creative energy to rush in and problems to rush out. Open, two-way communication makes everyone more effective.

SOLICIT R.F.P.
REQUEST COMPETITIVE INFO.
VIA REPS. ASAP.
(GIVE EMPLOYEE CREDIT)

<u>Are You *Really* Open to Feedback?</u>

Communication comes from the Latin word "commune," which means "held in common." To make communication work, we have to make sure that the people we're talking with understand what we're saying as well as we do. That means we must share enough information to bring them up to speed, and keep them informed about any changes that occur.

Including others requires thinking through and organizing our thoughts. It also means asking for feedback with statements like, "Tell me what your perception of this situation is," or "I want to know what you think about all this." If it's evident that others don't understand what we're saying, we must take the time to clarify and refine our message, realizing that other people's perspectives on life are different from our own. Doing all that may seem like a substantial investment of time and energy. I assure you it will take less than the time and energy required to deal with problems that result from lack of clear communication.

Pryor Resources, Inc. is known for teaching others to foster strong, two-way communication, yet sometimes I'm amazed by our own lack of it. Like many businesses, we believe in the need for open communication. But daily pressures and deadlines clog the lines, and, at times, communicating effectively with others becomes a difficult task.

How many times have you told the people who work for you that they can talk to you whenever they need to? But when someone comes to you with a problem, are you as responsive as you'd like to be? Have you responded with a brusque "Well, what do you want?" or "Hurry up, I don't have much time?" In essence, you've sent your employee two conflicting messages: "Talk to me; but not when I'm busy." Is there ever a time when you're not busy?

The next time people need help, chances are they won't come to you, but will seek assistance from peers who take the time to listen. That's a lot like the teenage girl who discovers she's pregnant. The first person she tells is a good friend. The last people she confides in are her parents. Why? Because she remembers how upset Mom and Dad got when she wrecked the car last summer—and wait until they see *this!* The conflicting message her parents have given her is: "Let us know any time you need our help, but don't come to us with problems. We've got too many of our own."

Much of how a person feels depends upon how he senses others feel about him—messages he receives both from their words and their actions. It's our responsibility to create an atmosphere in which people feel included, and feel free to express their opinions and needs. At Hallmark Cards, in one instance, a press operator declined to run a card because he believed it did not measure up to Hallmark's quality standards. Instead of reprimanding the pressman for delaying production, management valued his opinion and listened to what he had to say.

The Marriott Corporation takes a very direct approach to involving employees in communication. It's called the "Guarantee of Fair Treatment," and it's posted in every Marriott unit, which includes hotels, contract food services, and restaurants. This policy guarantees Marriott employees the right to bring their grievances right up through the organization until they are satisfied with the results. Since every manager is made aware of this policy and is obligated to follow it, it can cost the company a lot of executive time. But it's probably one of the main reasons Marriott is such a good place to work and consequently why it is such a successful hospitality company.

Marriott also keeps its lines of communication open with widespread use of "rap sessions" where employees get together and talk with senior executives. In talking with Bill Marriott, I was impressed with his commitment to continued participation in the organization. He, himself, will sit down with employees to talk. Consequently, all types of company modifications have resulted from these informal rap sessions.

To encourage the kind of participation and sensitivity to quality that are exhibited at Hallmark and Marriott, we have to work on a daily basis to build rapport with our work force. If we want our employees to display consistency, honesty, candor, and openness, we have to be able to exhibit those qualities ourselves.

Allowing for Others to Make Mistakes

One of the best ways you can encourage employees to help the organization reach its potential is to help your staff grow. At the same time you have to recognize and accept the fact that anyone who is learning and growing is occasionally going to make mistakes. Instead of chastising employees for their errors, help them understand what went wrong. Try to give them hope that their mistakes can be righted, and perhaps even point to mistakes you've made and lessons you learned from them. By being yourself with your employees and not putting on airs, you disclose part of yourself, letting others know you better.

If you're not happy with the way a supervisor completes performance evaluations of his employees, let him know how you feel about the problem rather than jumping all over him for causing it. You might say, "John, I'd like to talk with you about a frustration I have. I really believe in you, but I'm not comfortable with the way you are filling out your employee evaluation forms. I know they can be confusing; they caused me trouble at first, too. What can we do to make this process easier for you?" That way you're disclosing yourself. You're saying, "Look, I'm upset with the situation—but, hey, I've made the same mistake."

Learning to Speak Your Employees' Language Can Open a Whole New Dialogue

Sometimes managers need to step down from their soap-boxes and "speak the language" of their employees and share their experiences. If we do that, we may see that our perceptions of our employees may be very different from the reality.

Phil Love, president of Pryor Resources, Inc., did exactly that when employees in our Customer Service Department began asking for ways to make their jobs more interesting, advance their positions, and increase their earnings.

"Our employees in customer service had other goals in mind than working in Customer Service the rest of their lives," says Phil. "I really knew very little about their jobs, so I took some time to work in that department. I was trained to be a Customer Service representative, and each person in the department was responsible for teaching me certain aspects of my 'job.'

"In the process I learned a lot about each employee's organizational skills, job tasks, dreams, and frustrations. I also learned how articulate and intelligent they are. Most important, I realized that I had a lot of preconceived ideas about these associates. I learned that they have aspirations and drive, and are not just people passing time in front of a CRT screen handling orders for seminars. And I learned that they also had some assumptions about me as their leader that weren't true. Once we literally began working together, our perceptions changed, we understood each other better, and we communicated more effectively."

By getting out of his office and working with Customer Service employees, Phil saw that management and employees really wanted the same thing—to make valuable contributions and earn the satisfaction of a job well done. He began to see the strengths of employees in Customer Service, and was able to determine which other areas of the company they could work in to keep their interest alive and expand their career horizons.

Redistributing Energy Use During
Communication "Brownouts"

Do you know that we spend approximately 80 percent of our waking hours in some form of communication? It's estimated that 9 percent of that time is spent writing; 16 percent reading; 30 percent speaking; and 45 percent listening. But even though we devote so much time to communicating, 75 percent of the mistakes made in the workplace can be attributed to ineffective communication, and 80 percent of the business lost in America occurs because an employee communicates an attitude of indifference to a prospective customer or client.

I believe that one of the prime reasons for mis- or non-communication is employee "brownouts"—those times when people feel drained of energy and contributions suffer as a result. A manager who is in tune with her staff can identify when someone in her department is suffering from "brownout" by paying attention to how that person communicates. If an employee is apathetic in her responses or constantly complains, that could be an indication that she is overtaxed.

Just as we redistribute our use of energy when our community has an energy brownout, by doing laundry in the early morning before energy use is at its peak, we can also redistribute energy usage at work. Rather than cracking the whip over exhausted people, we can encourage them to take their vacations or participate in an exercise class.

Instead of letting their work and reputations suffer when they're tired, we must encourage employees to advocate their positions. First they need to listen to themselves—to monitor how they are feeling physically and mentally. Then they need to let us know if something has to change. They might say, "I'm really frustrated with this project. I need another employee to help me."

Another way to avoid "brownouts" is to encourage people in our organization to suggest improvements, rather than just registering complaints. Frederick S. (Fritz) Perls, father of Gestalt Psychology and author of *In and Out the Garbage Pail*

(Real People Press, 1969), stresses that "behind every bitch is a wish." That means that if your meal in a restaurant is served cold, you not only have a gripe, you also have a wish—you wish the food were warm. Employees and managers who learn to state their concerns or desires in the form of a wish will help avoid negative thinking.

Don't think that you have to deny the frustrations you feel with your job. Most people can sense when something isn't right, so let your feelings surface. Admit when something upsets you, but instead of just griping, let your wishes be known. Understand that, although everything can't be perfect all the time, the situation can improve if everyone is alerted to the problem and asked to help solve it.

As a manager, learn to tune into people's feelings and notice when something is out of kilter with them—even if they won't admit it. When employees feel they cannot trust management with their feelings, they begin to gripe to one another. If you begin hearing complaints, take immediate action. Suggest that you sit down and talk things out. Let employees know that you want to know how they feel, but that instead of just hearing complaints, you'd like to know how they'd like things to change. When you know what they're hoping for, you can begin to work out solutions.

Stamping Out Rumors: The Wisdom of Keeping Employees Informed

I believe that, when organizational problems are detected, managers should candidly explain the problems to employees, admit the stress, and be firm in conveying management's determination to make things better. Many people will remain loyal during tumultuous times if they are kept informed.

Let workers know that the company will survive, but that changes must be made. Employees should be given opportunities to make changes, but they should not have to be spoon-fed or coaxed into taking a bite out of the company's problems. If they don't want to get involved in helping the company, they shouldn't expect to be on board later, once the organization is sailing on smooth waters again.

At one major manufacturing company, for example, management realized that the incompetence of the secretarial staff played a major role in many of the company's problems. Instead of concealing this perception in the ivory tower of management and pruning down the secretarial staff one by one for "other" reasons, management held a meeting with the secretaries, including the head of the union. The company leaders gave the secretaries a choice—they could either improve their work, or kiss potential raises goodbye until they did.

The company agreed to provide the secretaries with the training they needed to come up to par, but the managers would not arrange the training classes—that was up to the secretaries themselves. If their jobs meant enough to them, they would work out the time and methods to increase their competency. And I'm pleased to report that that's exactly what happened.

It's Not What You Say, But How You Say It: Are Your Tone and Demeanor Speaking Well for You?

Remember how frustrated you got as a kid when you got in trouble for the way you spoke to someone—even when you didn't use foul language? When you tried to defend your innocence, your mother would scold, "It wasn't what you said, but the way you said it."

Well, Mom was right. Our demeanor, the tone of our voice, and the inflection we give to certain words all stem from our intentions (what's going on inside our head); and they directly affect how people perceive what we've said and how they will react to it.

If you're talking to me about something near and dear to you and I sit back in my chair eyeing the doodles I'm drawing, it won't be long before you sense my lack of interest. But if I stop what I'm doing, sit up, lean over the desk, and make eye contact, you'll know that my attention is directed at you and nowhere else.

Subtle messages-within-the-message are also dangerous. As a manager, I may want you to work overtime to get a project done. But instead of openly asking you to work the weekend, I tuck a hidden message into the conversation like, "I'll be looking at this report in my office on Sunday morning," or "You're going to be around Saturday, aren't you?"

These hidden messages abuse employees' good intentions. Since the manager is being tricky and coy, the employee often doesn't respond honestly, either. He may show up at work when he really feels he deserves time off, and be so angry that the quality of his work suffers. Or he may complain to others about the way you manipulate your staff. It would be better for everyone—including the workaholic manager—if the employee could admit that he feels frustrated that he is being asked to work when he really needs to rest and recharge.

One-on-one communication is difficult enough, but communicating to groups of people can be a nightmare of misunderstanding and unmet expectations. To get what we want from a meeting, we often need to turn up the volume of our presentations. If we want to get everyone's attention, we have to couple strong ideas with a strong personality. Instead of droning on in a monotone, we have to vary our facial expressions and the pitch of our voice. In other words, we have to present our ideas with excitement if we want to elicit excitement from others.

To make your ideas clearer and more emphatic when presenting to a group, list your points, succinctly stated, on handout sheets. If you are presenting facts or statistics, use graphs drawn on a flip chart or poster—but remember to talk to your audience, not to the flip chart. As you're speaking, ask questions to make sure everyone is following you; then answer their questions clearly and honestly. Try to avoid side issues to keep everyone focused on how "we" can do a better job together.

Problem-Solving with a Four-Step Gripebuster

What's your communication style? Do you foster communication or put others on the defensive and inflame their emotions? The most effective manager is one who asks for input and insight to solve problems, rather than using what he says to judge others and command action. The resourcing manager addresses issues specifically and asks the other people involved to help resolve problems. In short, he attacks issues, not people. He states how he feels with statements like, "I'm upset, I'm confused," and "I'm having difficulty understanding," rather than pointing the finger and blaming.

Take a minute to compare these two lists of effective and ineffective communication approaches:

Ineffective Approach	*Effective Approach*
Attacks people	Attacks problems
Uses negative labels	Avoids negative labels
Is very general	Is very specific

Now take a look at these lists to determine if your communication style is that of a controlling or resourcing manager:

The Controlling Manager	*The Resourcing Manager*
Pressures	Communicates
Judges	Offers feedback
Drives	Motivates
Rejects	Includes
Tells	Asks
Pushes	Challenges
Deflates	Inspires
Dictates	Negotiates

Here are some examples of how a controlling manager and a resourcing manager might say the same thing differently:

Controlling	*Resourcing*
"Here's what I want you to do…"	"Let's look at ways to…"

"I don't get involved in personal problems."	"If I help you with that, you'll be able to help me with this."
"We can't afford a copier."	"Let's see what it will take to justify one."
"Your production level is unsatisfactory."	"What can I do to make your job better?"
"I want that report by Friday."	"What do we need in order to get that ready by Friday?"
"I have to finish this letter by noon, so don't interrupt me."	"I need your help with ..."
"Why are you doing that?"	"Tell me about this project."

We are more effective when we work with other people to find solutions. When we misdirect blame onto other people rather than onto problems, we can easily fall into the trap of name-calling. And using negative labels like "slow" or "incompetent" makes it difficult to enlist the support of others when we need it later.

If a controlling manager felt that one of his employees continually lied about why work wasn't completed on time, he might say, "You're a liar; now tell me the truth."

But the resourcing manager, instead of labeling the employee as a dishonest person, thinks of him as a good person doing something bad. He shifts the focus from the person to the behavior. He may point to a specific incident when he believed the employee didn't tell the truth and say something such as, "I'm concerned about the accuracy of this statement." Or if he analyzed the situation, he might see that the employee must be under extraordinary pressure if he has to lie about unfinished work. Then he might ask the employee if he *does* feel a lot of pressure, and, if so, what he can do to help him or her.

Another communication blunder is giving feedback that is vague and general rather than specific and pointed. If I'm dissatisfied with a report someone on my staff wrote, I might generalize my feelings and say, "I don't like this report." When my employee says, "What didn't you like about it?" I respond with "I didn't like any of it." "What specifically?" the employee questions. "I'd change every bit of it," I snap, providing neither constructive criticism nor suggestions for improvement.

Or if a person missed a deadline, a controlling manager might demand, "*Why* wasn't this mailed yesterday?" This accusatory question would put the employee on the defensive. Not only would it make her feel like a failure, but it wouldn't address how to compensate for the missed deadline or how to avoid similar problems in the future.

A more effective approach would be to say, "Did you lack the information you needed to get this out on time? What can we do to be sure we meet deadlines in the future?"

Now what I've done is what one of my faculty members, Mike Murray, calls "changing gripes to goals." He suggests that we identify our frustrations, and then turn them into goal statements about how we would like things to be. So rather than feeling that she needs to defend herself against my accusation, my assistant is motivated to help accomplish our common goal.

The next time a problem comes up in your business, try this four-step "gripebuster:"

—My frustration is _____.
—What I would really like is _____.
—Therefore, my goal is _____.
—So the subject of this meeting is _____.

This technique avoids comments that make others feel diminished, and instead asks for their help in finding solutions.

What You Don't Say *Can* Hurt You: Nonverbals and Extra-Verbals Can Speak Louder than Words

At least 75 percent of any message is communicated nonverbally and in the tone of your voice (extra-verbally). If you present a new idea to a closed-minded person, he crosses his arms and locks his stance, creating a fortress that your ideas can't invade. Translated, this body language says, "Don't waste my time. I'm not going to like your ideas anyway."

To improve rapport through nonverbal communication, try a technique called mirroring—matching certain aspects of your behavior with those of the person you're talking to. Mirroring doesn't mean mimicking, nor is it manipulative; it is an attempt to establish a connection for mutual benefit. Here are three mirroring techniques that can help you enhance communication:

—Match your voice tone or tempo with the other person's. If he or she talks rapidly, try picking up your pace somewhat.

—Mirror movement rhythms. If a person moves slowly and you move quickly, consider slowing down.

—Pay attention to body posture. Watch a couple on a date. If one smiles, the other smiles. Now observe how you react in situations where you have the greatest rapport. If the other person leans against the doorway, you lean against the other side of the doorway. But if you feel hostile toward someone, you probably act as differently as possible.

Try to stay aware of your nonverbal communication and how it could affect others. Changing the way you stand or the intonation of your voice could make a big difference in the way others perceive you and how well they hear what you're trying to say.

Opening Up About Cover-Ups: How to Keep the Work Force Informed About Confidential Information

When leaders are about to implement major changes within an organization, many try to keep the information classified for as long as possible so as not to alarm the work force. But sooner or later, news of the changes is bound to leak out to people. Hearing only part of the story stirs up free-floating anxiety among employees, causing the rumor mill to begin turning.

Instead of hushing up news of the changes in the first place, and having to deny the rumors later, managers can do the following: First, be frank about the proposed changes and reasons behind them. Then let employees express whatever anxiety they might feel in open discussion, and respond candidly to their concerns. Secrecy is sometimes warranted—for instance, in the acquisition of another company—so employees should know that they may not be privy to all the facts. But give them as much specific, accurate information as possible. Once the worries are out in the open and employees feel they are receiving what information you can provide, the rumors will quiet down.

At Donnelly Corporation, a Holland, Michigan, mirror and glass product manufacturer that's responsible for nearly all the rear-view mirrors found in American automobiles, managers don't try to hide information from their 1,200 employees. Instead, they make a point of keeping the work force informed. "We make a significant effort to communicate the realities of business to our employees, through frequent group meetings between our employees and top management from various business groups, and through focus meetings attended by both management and representatives from each work team," says Jim Knister, vice president and chief financial officer of the company.

"During the workteam meetings, employees may bring up problems with quality control, ask why certain equipment or tools have not been ordered, or discuss cooperation issues with other departments. Sometimes people may be put on the spot, but in an open communication system, people have the right to say what they need to a variety of people. That makes the probability of *getting* what they need a lot higher. In a conventional management system an issue may stop at the boss's desk, and an employee would have nowhere else to turn. In an open communication system, there are many options and many ways an employee can be heard.

"We believe that employees who are economically literate and knowledgeable about business, quality measures, and customer satisfaction do a better job," continues Knister. "During the monthly focus groups the president of the company talks about general business conditions and what is happening in the various markets we serve. We believe in people at Donnelly, and we try to communicate that to them. And the results have been excellent. Our employees are hardworking and loyal, and turnover and absenteeism are very low."

If You Listen Closely, You'll Discover Three Types of Learners: Which One Are You?

Do you sometimes wish that the people you are talking to had antennae for ears so they could pick up all the signals you're transmitting? There have always been contests and prizes for the "best speaker." But we might want to add to that an award for the "best listener." To see how valued the winner of that award would be, ask yourself: "Who would I rather have as an employee or boss—the best speaker or the best listener? And who would I rather live with the rest of my life—a champion talker or a good listener?

A good listener commands high worth—modern-day psychiatry attests to that. Many relationship breakups are traceable to communication breakdowns. There's usually a lot of talking but not much listening. As Leo Buscaglia, Ph.D., once said, "Most conversations are just alternating monologues—the question is, is there any real listening going on?" In most cases, there's not. People don't like to listen because it interferes with their talking.

When engaged in a conversation, remember to participate actively rather than passively observing. Active listening keeps our mind from wandering and increases our concentration. The word "attention" means a series of tensions. One of the best ways to involve yourself in a conversation is to ask questions. The quality of your questions often determines the quality of the answer you receive. Don't just ask shallow yes-or-no questions, which give back limited information. Opt for probing, open-ended questions that give the other person an opportunity to express himself. That type of searching question will show your employees that you truly are interested in what they say and that their ideas and opinions really count.

Also pay attention to how employees respond to what you say. By listening to the comments they make, you can tell what type of learners they are. Some people, for example, are "visual." They need to see something done before they understand it. Their conversation will be characterized by visual words, such as, "I see."

Other employees are "auditory." They need to hear detailed explanations before they can understand something. Their conversation will include words such as, "It sounds good to me," or "I hear you."

Still a third group is called "kinesthetic." This means they need a physical understanding of things because they are "hands-on" learners. They don't get the most from explanations, and they don't benefit too much from watching you do something. It's not until you let them try to do something themselves that they will comprehend fully. Their conversations contain phrases such as, "That doesn't feel right," or "Let's develop a hands-on approach now."

People enjoy learning, but we have to be clear about what we want to teach them, and teach it in the way they can understand best.

Through creative, active listening, we exercise an almost magical skill that makes other people feel important, and relationships grow strong. In the ancient Bible story, King Solomon was offered any gift he named. He asked for "a listening heart." The king knew way back then what the greatest leaders of the world have known right up to our day—that all real listening is done with the heart and stimulates wisdom.

Yes, but . . .

Yes, I agree with the need to listen, but how can I handle an employee whose mind continually wanders

when I give instructions? He doesn't even pay attention when I tell him how important it is to listen!

We like to think that as soon as we address an issue with someone that should be the end of a problem. It takes anywhere from nine to 18 months to integrate a new skill into our lives.

Keep letting your employee know how you feel and praise him when he does listen. Help him to concentrate by asking him questions when you give him directions. In other words, make it a discussion between the two of you. Ask him what he thinks of the plan and if there are any changes he'd like to make. An employee who values his job and your impressions of him will do all he can to concentrate and take an active part in the discussion.

Yes, as a manager I try to give my employees all the information they need to do their jobs, but how can I get my boss to give me feedback? He seldom tells me whether or not he likes my work or management style.

Often getting what you want is simply a matter of asking for it. If you need feedback, help structure an environment that will encourage it. Ask your boss for periodic performance reviews. Tell him you would like to discuss what expectations you both have and set some goals. Let him know that in two months you would like to review your progress toward these goals. Rather than just a nebulous complaint, you will be providing your own solution instead of saddling him with both the problem and the solution.

CHAPTER 8

Maximizing Energy:
Discovering Strength
in Numbers

Many businesspeople are seeing the need to turn away from the "prima donna" attitude—the belief that we have to "do it on our own"—and to move toward an interactive approach built on teamwork. Some of the most successful managers are the ones who encourage employees to work together cooperatively. These managers have seen the synergy that results when employees are able to share ideas and resources. And they've witnessed how the momentum they've gained from the cooperative spirit helps move them along more quickly and efficiently toward their goal.

For years we have tended to try to act the "hero"—the self-reliant person who never asks for help. And we've encouraged the same tendency in the people who work for us. Employees in the typical organization have been more likely to compete with their peers for the spotlight than to ask for help, because that has been seen as a sign of weakness.

Just take a minute to imagine this scene: you've been put in charge of the purchasing department of your organization, and the president tells you the purchasing procedures need to be rewritten. What would you do? Chances are you would go to your office and rewrite the purchasing procedures all by yourself—believing that since you're the specialist in that area, you should know what's best for the company.

You develop a new system and the president approves it. But within a few days, other employees start tromping into the president's office to complain about what you've done. You've neglected to ask other people in the company how your design would affect their department—so it's no wonder the new system doesn't meet their approval. You've wasted a lot of people's time and energy by not viewing things on a systemwide basis, and by not anticipating the needs of others with whom you work. You've isolated yourself from others and expected maximum results—an almost-impossible outcome.

Maintaining the Excitement of a Task Force for Everyday Tasks: W.L. Gore & Associates Is a Case-in-Point

The changes you make in your approach to managing will have a ripple effect on those around you. The company W. L. Gore & Associates is a case in point.

A couple of years ago I had the opportunity to spend some time with Wilbert L. Gore, who has since passed away, and I asked him about the lattice structure of his company. He said that one of the goals of his company was to eliminate authority figures who made decisions autocratically. When I asked him why he had created a system without a defined organizational structure, he told me he was inspired by the task forces he served on when he was in the Army and when he worked for DuPont.

"When people were on a task force, they were so excited about their work you couldn't *make* them go home," said Gore. "Within a task force everyone was equal. There was no pressure from 'higher up,' and everyone had permission to talk to everyone else. But when employees went back to their non-task-force, day-to-day activities, the team spirit disappeared and energy dissipated. I wanted to create a company in which people had the freedom to brainstorm and work as a team on a daily basis, not just when they were assigned to a special committee."

Because "all employees are created equal" at W.L. Gore, associates are not embarrassed to ask for feedback—in fact, they're expected to do so. Allowing people to bounce ideas off one another and share resources has become the company's built-in checks and balances system.

W.L. Gore & Associates is partially owned by its own work force, so people feel especially comfortable sharing ideas with one another. But the same spirit can exist within *any* organization that doesn't rely solely on one individual's judgment.

When we hire new associates at Pryor Resources, Inc., we tell them, regardless of their position, that their first job is to be part of the management team, and their second job is the one described in their job description. From the first day on the job, employees know that they are managers, resources and assets to the company, and that their contributions—on *any* topic, whether or not it pertains to their particular job—are both welcomed and desired.

Working in the interactive environment we have at Pryor Resources enables our employees to give their best to the company. They can capitalize on their strengths, and they know they can get help from others in their weaker areas; so they feel good about their contributions, and the entire organization benefits. Our people feel confident asking for feedback and trying new alternatives. Even if a new idea ultimately doesn't work, the individual hasn't risked his reputation, and no one thinks less of him; his effort is applauded, in fact.

In a noninteractive company, on the other hand, workers often tend to believe that there is a substantial difference between what other people *want* them to do and what they actually *can* do. So they feel threatened, and contribute less. For example, if you expect me continually to have brilliant new ideas,

I'll probably be so preoccupied with the fear of failure that I'll be too paralyzed to share *any* of my ideas with you. I'll make better contributions when you help me feel that my input is appreciated and that other associates will work to support or enhance my ideas, regardless of whether they're fully polished gems or diamonds in the rough.

At Stew Leonard's Dairy It's Not <u>What</u> They Sell, but <u>How</u> They Sell It

Stew Leonard, owner of Stew Leonard's Dairy Store in Norwalk, Connecticut, finds that the good will created among employees who work together synergistically in his organization is passed along to store customers. Leonard owns what has been called the "World's Largest Dairy Store," an amazing place that boasts more sales per square foot than any other retail store in the world. Some 100,000 customers shop at Stew Leonard's each week, and when I saw the store and met the staff, I knew why.

The dairy store has a show-biz atmosphere that makes pushing a grocery cart down the aisle as much fun as maneuvering an electric car at Disneyland. In fact, Leonard says he has intentionally modeled himself after the late Walt Disney. He likes to capitalize on good feelings, knowing that happy customers make cash registers ring.

The dairy store is bright and full of fascinating things to see and do. When customers arrive at the parking lot, they're greeted by a petting zoo filled with chickens, geese and goats and watched over by a security guard decked out in farmer's duds. Inside the store, there's a mechanical chicken that lays artificial eggs; and there are employees dressed as barnyard animals and cartoon characters who roam the aisles entertaining the kids. Children often beg their parents to stop at Stew Leonard's, but even adults can't help smiling when they shop at the dairy store. Result? The average customer shops there twice a week and spends an average of $50 per visit!

True, maybe it's the helium balloons and the smell of freshly baked croissants that attract people to the store to begin with. But Leonard says it's not what he sells but the way his employees sell it that keeps customers coming back. Competitors come from around the world to look for Leonard's secret to success. They take note of the single horseshoe-shaped aisle that winds through his store, study how his products are displayed, and compare his prices to their own.

"If they would just ask me for the secret, I'd tell them," says Leonard. "We're successful because of the interest and care that my employees take with each customer."

Shirley and I felt that Stew Leonard's employees were genuinely interested in us. They went out of their way to show us around their store; and as we watched and listened to them, we could sense the synergy in Stew Leonard's organization from their cheerful voices and effervescent chitchat. A security guard drove us to Stew Leonard's home, where the former milkman shared his philosophy with me about what it takes to create an energetic organization.

"Just like people, an organization has a personality," Leonard said, "and customers can sense that personality the minute they walk through the door. Our employees don't bark orders at each other or question their responsibility. In fact, they almost have a sixth sense about what they need to do to maximize the store's effectiveness."

Leonard told me a story about his daughter, Beth, who created and manages Bethy's Bakery at her father's store. When the company was looking for someone to fill a position in another department, Beth suggested one of her own bakery employees for the promotion.

"She did that even though she knew that replacing one of her best employees would be rough on her department," explained Leonard. "Beth was excited for her employee and, like all of our employees, she has a natural tendency to do what is most beneficial for the company as a whole. That's the kind of team spirit we pride ourselves on."

After our visit with Stew Leonard, a security guard drove us back to the train station. Knowing we were pressed for time (we had to get back to New York in time to get to the airport and make our flight home), he took us on a shortcut through back streets. And he assured us that if we missed our train he'd drive us to the next town to catch another. It was because of that guard's extra efforts that we arrived at the station with one minute to spare.

That's the kind of energetic spirit—that "something extra"—that all of Stew Leonard's employees exhibit. It's evident that their eagerness to please is an extension of Stew Leonard's adherence to his golden rule—treat others as you would want to be treated.

To be sure that new employees at Stew Leonard's will add to, not detract from, the store's chemistry, job candidates are rated on a scale of one to ten. Only the employees who rate a "ten" are selected. Leonard says his company looks for outgoing, gregarious employees who will work together synergistically. And once he selects those employees, he is able to keep them for years. Many dairy store employees have worked there for more than 20 years; some have gone away to college and then come back to the store to fill positions with more responsibility. And generations of the same family have all earned their living at the store. Stew Leonard's employees remain loyal, energetic, and hardworking because they feel they belong to a "family" that will help them overcome obstacles and support them in their efforts to succeed.

Four Steps to Increase Synergy: It All Starts with You

How do you develop a network of employees who are as committed and loyal as Stew Leonard's people? What does it take to get employees to give you honest feedback? How do you get your employees to support and encourage each other, to help smooth the highs and lows of the workday?

Step One: Change your attitude

The first step to creating a support system may be a tough one for some managers. Here's what you have to do: you have to honestly believe that no matter how high up in the company you are, you can benefit from what others have to give.

Step Two: Start by supporting others

Once you accept the fact that you don't have all the answers and need help from others, the second step to creating a support system is to be supportive to others. Here are a few suggestions for how to build that support:

—Take time to talk to people.

—Find a few minutes to share information, and offer suggestions.

—Show an interest in what your people are saying and doing.

—Step out of your office and take time to get involved in professional organizations or enroll in seminars where you can hear new ideas and build new relationships.

Remember that the office isn't the only place you can practice being supportive. In fact, one of the best places to begin being supportive is at home—with your friends or your spouse and your kids. Can you put down the paper and listen to what others have to say about their day? Will you take time this weekend to watch your son's baseball game or ask your daughter why she didn't try out for cheerleader when she had said she wanted to?

Step Three: Ask others to help you

Once you have become supportive of others, you can begin asking people to help *you*. Look for people who are honest and direct; realize that your knowledge base and effectiveness will increase dramatically when you begin paying attention to what others say and do.

Many people say that as they move up the ladder of success, their support systems tend to weaken. That's because the higher we climb, the less we talk to others about our feelings. It's difficult to open up to our subordinates knowing that discussing issues with those our decisions may directly affect can be unwise. It may also imply a lack of confidence in our ability to manage effectively alone.

To get help wrestling with management problems, top managers often look outside their companies to external support systems, joining associations or study groups. They turn to groups like the Young Presidents' Organization and the Southern California group, Tech, a club for company executives. Or they may get expert help with problems in specific areas: external support systems you can turn to include attorneys, marketing specialists, and executive consultants.

Some people I've talked with say they have difficulty with this last alternative. Suppose you want to hire a consultant or buy a new piece of equipment to help maximize your performance, but you're required beforehand to get a go-ahead from your boss or the board of directors. What can you do? Here's a tip: when you tell the authority you need assistance, keep the focus on the benefit to the organization. If you've purchased new software for your computer but aren't getting the desired results, don't say to your boss, "I want to hire a software consultant." Instead, try, "How would you like to get someone in here who can help us get a better return on our investment in computer software?" Remember, there's power in words—and they must be chosen carefully.

Step Four: Start to support yourself

Above all, become your own internal support system. Keep a steady flow of positive self-talk going on inside of you at all times. Feed yourself healthy emotional groceries that will give you the confidence you need to give support to others and to ask for their support.

Composing the Right Employee Mix: Don't Just Look for Carbon Copies

To build a synergistic employee team, you'll need to choose the right "mix" of people. Traditionally, leaders have hired carbon copies of themselves, but today more and more business leaders are looking for individuals who aren't clones—who have strengths different from their own. They want employees whose personalities, workstyles, and skills will complement one another. As a result, they are now paying more attention to the personality mix within their organizations. They may look for one person who pays attention to details, another who is a questioner, and another who is a doer.

At W.L. Gore & Associates, managers put prospective employees through multiple interviews to ensure that the candidates will "fit" into the company. Gore said that the selection process is fundamental to the success of an organization, and that taking the extra hours to hand-pick employees is well worth the time investment.

A while back my company hired a new marketing specialist whose workstyle is different from that of other key managers. But in this case, that's exactly what we wanted. This new manager is detail-oriented, while our other managers are conceptualists, and we welcome the balance. Note, though, that while his workstyle is different from ours, he shares common values that are essential to our company. He's involved, willing to work, excited about new goals, and oriented positively toward change. He's also committed to equality and not to a hierarchical, authoritative structure. We hired him for his differences and his similarities, and we used information we'd gained through numerous interviews and interactions to determine that he and our organization were right for each other.

Using Intuition to Select Staff Members

Management books and training seminars will give you dozens of scientific models of personality styles, which may help you identify the types of employees who will work together well and the types who are right for a specific job. However, one of the most important, and perhaps most overlooked, tools is our intuition—our sixth sense that tells us how we feel when we interact with someone.

As I mentioned earlier, most women—my wife Shirley included—have refined intuitive capacities and feel freer than men do about relying on their intuition to help make important decisions. Women in business need reinforcement to use their intuitive abilities and men need encouragement to further develop theirs. Here are some tips for using your own "sixth sense" more effectively.

Get in touch with your own feelings. Too often, we let our intuition become obstructed because we are impressed by a person's credentials or experience. But instead of thinking about a candidate's background, pay attention to how you feel about him on a personal level. Ask yourself questions about the way he presents himself and what he wants from the job. Is he coming on too strong or trying to make himself look too good? Has he said he's more qualified than what he is? Does he seem controlling or manipulative?

Check your "gut feelings" about the candidate. If your intuition tells you that the person's personality will fit, ask questions about workstyle to see if it will mesh with the other people he will work with and with the company's overall philosophy. At Pryor Resources, Inc., we like employees who are "free-floating" and aren't dependent on structure. We've hired a few employees who liked to be pigeon-holed in tight compartments, but they haven't fitted in well and have seemed constantly frustrated. When an employee doesn't "fit" our organization, our natural tendency is to develop bad feelings about him; but what we should do, instead, is simply recognize that synergistically he wasn't well-placed, and either consider relocating him within the company or helping him move on to an organization in which his style will fit.

Training and Development: The Bottom Line in Human Resources Accounting

Hiring employees who fit in well with your organization is just one step toward becoming a truly "synergetic" manager. The next step, once you have your employees on board, is to enhance their strengths and help them overcome their weaknesses by giving them plenty of opportunities for training and development. If you encourage them to continue their education, you can help them upgrade their skills—and you may find that their attitudes change positively, too. Most important, you'll make them into more valuable members of *your* team.

Just as we pay close attention to the bottom line in financial accounting, we need to stay aware of the bottom line in "human resources accounting." Human resources are our most valuable commodity, yet some organizations consider continuing education programs an unnecessary expenditure, instead of looking at them as an investment. We often purchase maintenance contracts to keep up our equipment and insure that it functions properly, but we may not make the same type of investment in our people. We must change our thinking on this. We live in an age when technology is changing rapidly and new information is readily available—in fact, I've heard that if a person earned a doctorate degree in a technical field in 1970, up to 98 percent of what he learned is no longer accurate today. Just to keep up, our employees must have ongoing training and development. Investing in employees this way pays back huge dividends. They feel better about themselves, they're more knowledgeable, and they're more capable of making contributions to the organization.

But it's easy for employees to feel that they're so busy they can't afford to spend time taking seminars and classes. I remember the time I used the excuse of not having enough time to attend a time management seminar, only to realize that learning to use my time effectively was exactly why I needed to go! There's an old story that speaks to this issue quite well. It goes like this: There were once two men who worked all day sawing down trees. One sawed nonstop without a break; the other sawed for a while, then took time to sit down and sharpen his saw. By the end of the day, the man who had periodically stopped to sharpen his blade achieved more than the one who worked continually. The moral to the story? We'll get more done and in a more efficient manner if we learn to work smart, not just work hard. The rewards will be greater if we take time to sharpen the tools we work with—our minds—than if we work continuously and let our minds grow dull. You, the energetic manager, must push your employees to keep their minds and skills sharp—that way you'll end up with a truly major-league team.

The Hard Lesson of Learning to Play

What I've just said applies most of all to *you*—the team leader.

Do you take pride in working hard? Is finding time on your calendar for a jog around the park or a weekend in the mountains like trying to squeeze an extra piece into a jigsaw puzzle? Do you tend to focus continually on what you have to tackle next, rather than taking a few minutes to enjoy what you've succeeded in accomplishing?

The dictionary defines "success" as the achievement of a goal. Do you realize that some people achieve next to nothing and still manage to feel wonderful? Have you ever been around a sleep-till-nooner who for once wakes up at 10 a.m. and stands at the top of the stairs and through a big-toothed smile exclaims, "I'm up!"

Isn't it amazing? It's 10 a.m. and already he considers himself an overachiever. You've been up since before dawn and have only completed about one-third of what you thought you would. Even though you've been working for hours, you consider yourself a failure. He just got up and already he's ahead of the game! Do you know that the chances are nine in ten that he's going to attend your funeral? And there's about the same chance that he's going to inherit everything you own.

Think about how different your definition of success is from his. His goal of the day was just to get up before noon, and since he accomplished that goal, he's a winner. But you, as an overachieving perfectionist, are always trying to do more—so no matter how much you get done, it's not enough.

It's easy to become so task-oriented that we lose sight of the big picture and forget to pat ourselves on the back for what we've done to help reach our goals. It's to our advantage not only to work hard but also to work *smart*, and to take time to rest after a job well done.

Why Rest and Relaxation Are Essential

It's one of the laws of human nature: after performing a certain amount of work, we are definitely going to regress. It often happens like this. You're normally a cool, level-headed, rational person. But after working intensely for a long period of time without a break, you become irritable, critical, and childlike. What can you do about this? Don't continue to ignore the fact that you will become less effective if you work yourself to a frazzle and don't take time to rejuvenate. Instead, plan for the law of diminishing returns, and plan to take steps—if not to prevent fatigue, at least to cope with it. You can do that by scheduling some time for yourself—away from work. By letting the child within you "out to play," you will nourish that part of yourself and be able to go back to work feeling refreshed.

Several years ago, NASA conducted a study to determine how people worked most effectively. They had groups of people work for eight hours before taking a one-hour break, work for four hours before taking a two-hour break, work two hours with a one-hour break, and work for an hour breaking a minute or two throughout the hour. The study showed conclusively that working with regular intermittent breaks produced long-term energy and higher efficiency. If people could relax periodically by laughing, joking, and playing, they could actually work more intensely, precisely, and thus efficiently.

Planning a Health and Fitness Program
for Your Employees

In addition to being unhealthy, overworking is not as fashionable or as impressive as it once was! People who kept alert with strong black coffee and coped with stress by lighting up a cigarette used to be hailed as "company men" who knew their priorities. But today, many business managers are realizing that the employees who give their best are the ones who take time to exercise, pay attention to their diet, have kicked health-draining habits like smoking and drinking, and have taken up exercising and enjoying life a bit instead.

An ever-growing number of Fortune 500 companies have built gymnasiums on-site for their employees. Other progressive companies offer free annual physicals and send top management on weekend "getaways" to unwind. Energetic managers know that employees perform better when their lives are in balance. With the high cost of health care insurance and hospitalization, keeping employees healthy and happy actually saves businesses money.

In my company, I have found that caring about my employees' lifestyles and not just their workstyles has given them a sense of loyalty to the company that raises or bonuses can't buy. Working with a local hospital, we are providing a wellness program that includes complete physicals, stress reduction training, aerobic exercise, a smoking cessation program, and cooking/nutrition classes.

I've received cards from employees thanking me for caring about them as people—not just workers. One woman, who was out of shape, told me how grateful she was for the aerobics class we offer. Another woman on our salesforce was able to spot a tumor in an early stage; she said she probably wouldn't have noticed it on her own for some time. Veteran smokers tell me that they've been able to quit or control their smoking, and are spending less money on cigarettes and feeling better than they have in years. And now instead of bringing candy and cookies to office parties, associates are making fruit and vegetable snacks, using the information they've gained through the nutrition courses. They are feeling better, and they're putting their increased energy back into the company by working with more vigor and commitment.

I encouraged the wellness program because of a personal commitment I have made to a healthy lifestyle. Eating a diet low in sugar and salt, free of caffeine, and with limited amounts of meat, has helped me at age 53 to maintain a busy work and travel schedule that would exhaust some people in their twenties. When we started the wellness program at Pryor Resources, Inc., I was excited about sharing these lifestyle principles with others but I wasn't convinced that they would benefit the business. Today I know that the program has paid for itself.

But even though wellness programs and exercise gymnasiums are proving successful with employees at some companies, we shouldn't think that being benevolent allows us to manipulate our employees. If such programs are initiated for economic reasons only, employees will know it right away, and the programs will lack the spirit they need to make them successful. If we want to employ people who care about the organization, we have to begin by caring for and about them. People dedicate their energies to something when their hearts are truly in it, not when they've been coaxed or prodded.

How "Play Breaks" Can Improve Your Decision-Making

Taking a time-out from work will help you gain new insights into old problems. While your body and mind are concentrating on some diversion, whether it's playing racquetball or watching your favorite hockey team race toward the goal, your subconscious may be working out solutions to your most pressing work problems. Or while you're sailing on a catamaran, you may realize that the issue that was causing you so much stress and concern isn't as important as it seemed at the time.

In 1985, I held a management retreat for my staff at a Colorado ski resort. One afternoon, we began discussing some complicated issues that were causing problems within our company. My normal tendency would have been to stay at the meeting and work until the problem was resolved. But instead, when the time came for our afternoon break, I kept a date to meet several colleagues on the ski slopes.

I was the least experienced—and the most naive—skier in

the group. So, when the others suggested that we ski down a certain slope, I readily agreed, having no idea that it was the steepest ski run of all. For the next two hours, that mountain got my complete concentration. There was no way I could think about the meeting or anything else when I felt as though my life were on the line—and when I got to the bottom of the mountain, I realized it had been! The diversion of skiing kept my conscious mind involved so that my subconscious could gain perspective on the business issues at hand.

When I returned to the lodge that afternoon I breezed into the conference room with renewed energy—and was surprised to find a few people still hunched over the conference table drinking melted ice, locked into a repetition of our afternoon's discussion.

After conquering that monstrous snow-covered mountain, the work-related problem no longer appeared as treacherous to me, and, in fact, it seemed surmountable. By getting away and "letting my child out to play," I had thought of solutions for how to resolve the situation. That evening, when we reconvened the meeting, my new-found energy rubbed off on others. Not only did we resolve the immediate problem, but we accomplished all our other objectives as well.

That experience proved to me how essential it is to get away from our work. If we don't take the time to unwind and give our minds a break, we will not have the sharpness of mind we need to make good business decisions. We cannot expect the most from ourselves during worktime if we don't allow ourselves time to regroup.

You Are What You Have Been Becoming: How You Live Today Maps Your Future

Have you ever stopped to realize that each day makes a substantial difference in who you will be tomorrow. If you want to be active and vibrant at age 70, you had better start by leading a healthy life today. And that goes for your business career *and* personal life.

Ask yourself this: is your mental self-image today one you'll be proud of next year or five years from now? While your values at age 50 may be somewhat different from those you had at 30, chances are you don't want to live your life wishing you had done things differently—wishing you had paid more attention in college and partied less, or that you had spent more time with the kids when they were young and less time at work. The problem with the Epicurean philosophy, "Eat, drink, and be merry, for tomorrow we may die," is that we don't die tomorrow. We have to live with the person we've been becoming. Therefore, we must be accountable for our actions and behavior today.

When I was speaking at a Young Presidents Organization, Inc. (YPO) conference held in San Diego, I met a man who was a perfect example of someone who is proud of what he's become—in both his business and personal life. At just this side of 80, J.R. Simplot is one of the wealthiest people in America. In 1922, at age 14, he left home and supported himself by collecting pigs during a time when pork prices dropped radically and farmers were selling their pigs at low, low prices or giving them away because they didn't want the cost of feeding them. Within a few months, Simplot had hundreds of pigs and he took care of them for months until pork was in demand again and he was able to sell them for $7,800—which made him a rich young man still in his teens. With that money Simplot got into the potato processing business, and by 1940 he had 1,000 people working for him. Simplot became known as "Mister Spud" a name given to him after he developed the frozen french fry and convinced Ray Kroc to use those fries in McDonald's restaurants across the country.

Today, Simplot remains a gutsy entrepreneur. Although he earned most of his fortune in the potato processing business, he is now into a more exotic enterprise—the making of semiconductor chips for computers. Simplot is still actively involved in his businesses, which have gross sales of more than $1 billion a year. What is his secret? Has he found his own fountain of youth? You might say so.

Simplot is a high-energy person. While many people at his age feel fortunate just to be able to get out of the chair to change the television station, Simplot and his wife were out jogging the morning before the conference began. And when YPO members went to a Beach Boys concert, Simplot showed up too, complete with a hand-held television that would let him keep track of the World Series. Simplot has not lost the vitality and excitement he had when he made his first fortune as a teenager. His life is balanced and his mind is alert. He is what he has been becoming. He is his own self-fulfilling prophecy.

Yes, but...

If you're not yet convinced that creating support systems, building a synergistic environment, and providing a balanced lifestyle for yourself *and* your employees can make you a more truly energetic manager, let me try to persuade you further. Perhaps you are saying:

—"Yes, but I think to run an organization most efficiently employees need direction and strong leadership."

It's been my experience that employees contribute more when they are convinced that what they say and do matters. The old image of the all-knowing, untouchable leader is passe and, in fact, it polarizes relationships in an organization.

Many managers used to believe that only a few of their people had the answers and that the magic key to success was in the systems they created. But now, progressive managers are realizing that good employees are not "a dime a dozen." It takes the dedication of all employees to create the success we desire.

To me, leadership is not something that can be appointed. People follow someone who has earned the right to be their leader. W.L. Gore said that in task forces, leaders emerge because they have the competency and skills that make others want to follow them. One way we earn the right to lead other people is by helping those people to maximize their potential. When people feel good about what they are getting from us, they will give more to us in return.

And then you may be saying to yourself,

—"Why should I concern myself with support systems, synergy, and wellness programs? What happened to the good old days, when we just hired someone and expected him to do the job?"

We're living in a different era today than the "good old days" you remember. Just as we fly on streamlined 747 jets and not outdated prop planes, we need to use the best, most up-to-date techniques to run our businesses.

People may have done their jobs well in the past, but they worked with less personal satisfaction. Dissatisfaction led to the formation of unions, mistrust of management, and hatred of bosses. People who barked orders at work, barked orders at home. Our culture drove people to alcohol, drugs, and disillusionment; caused others to die young from heart attacks and hypertension; and helped the divorce rate to soar.

I believe that managers who encourage a healthy, balanced lifestyle will create a more satisfied, productive work force. And the good news is that the "trickle down" effect is at work and some of our most strongly humanistic organizations are spawning other great companies. An example of that is Jimmy Treybig, who started Tandem Computer, Inc., based on the positive experiences he had while working at Hewlett-Packard. As more and more managers pattern themselves after business leaders who truly care about their employees, more and more people in this country will reap the benefits.

CHAPTER 9

Tapping New Energy Sources: Mining the Wealth of Creativity and Innovation Within Your Organization

During the energy crisis of the early 1970s, it became strikingly apparent that new energy sources had to be developed. Government and private industry alike began searching for alternative ways of creating energy.

One project that resulted from that search is the Power Tower, a solar energy research project in Albuquerque, New Mexico. This 200-foot-tall tower is used primarily to test the feasibility and advance the technology of the solar central receiver concept. The idea behind that concept is to use giant, computer-controlled mirrors to track the sun. The reflection from the mirrors is focused into a receiver on top of a tower and the energy collected is used to boil water. This creates steam, which is then used to generate electricity.

This project is a perfect illustration of an important point about energy: We rarely create new sources of energy for our world, we simply tap existing ones. The same is true when it comes to the individuals and organizations you manage. You don't need to look for new sources of energy. They're right there at your fingertips. They're in your people, your systems, your technology and your markets. But it takes creativity and innovation to tap them and reach their full potential.

Exploding the Creativity Myth of "Some Have It, Some Don't"

To me, creativity means doing ordinary things in extraordinary ways. It's seeing what everyone else sees, but thinking what no one else thinks. Ed Cunningham of Hallmark Cards, Inc. defines creativity in more earthy terms in an essay in the company's 1984 Corporate Report:

> It's an urge to build, as compelling as the urge to mate, an instinct to explore, as essential as the instinct to survive. It's a hunger to grow, a drive to renew, a thirst to understand our world, a craving to complete ourselves.

I believe that the opposite of creativity is conformity. If we're busy conforming, we are not thinking of how to do things in an easier, better, or bigger way. There is the story about the young couple who was fixing their first Thanksgiving dinner. When the wife cut off both ends of the turkey, the husband asked, "Why did you do *that*, honey?" "I don't know, but my Mom always cooked turkey this way. Let's ask her." The woman called her mother. "I don't know," said the mother, "but that's the way my mother always did it. Ask Grandma." So she did, and Grandma replied, "Why, that's the only way I could get the bird into the tiny oven we had."

We're too often eager to follow other people's leads without asking ourselves if there could be a better way. In the business world, one of the greatest stiflers of creativity is bureaucracy. In that type of compartmentalized environment, word comes down from the top explaining how something should be done, and no one thinks or dares to question why. But while rules and regulations have their places, so do creativity and innovation.

Some people, like Ed Cunningham of Hallmark Cards, Inc., paint creativity as a universal ingredient to which we all have access; others see it in a "some have it, some don't" light. Creativity has always had certain misleading and unfair stereotypes associated with it. It's thought only to belong to Bohemian artists, crazed scientists, and obsessed computer nerds. It's considered a gift only bestowed on a chosen few.

Unfortunately, the intangible quality of creativity lends itself to this form of typecasting, as Cunningham explains in the opening to his essay:

> Some have labeled it a process like sausage making, while others think of it as an inherited condition like freckles. Some have placed it on a pedestal called "genius" or worshiped it at a shrine named "divine inspiration"...Such has been the history of creativity, that elusive force about which so much has been said and so little understood.

Such stereotypes have made it difficult for the average person, whose painting masterpiece is done in latex on the toolshed, to believe that he has what it takes to be creative. Often when I ask people if they consider themselves creative, the immediate answer is "no." They tell me that creativity belongs in the domain of New York's Soho District or in their company's research and development department.

Creativity is not reserved for the "gifted" or the wild-haired artists. It belongs to anyone who can "see" novel associations that are useful. The simple Post-it (TM) Note idea developed by Art Frye at 3M of backing the top of small sheets of paper with low-tack adhesive so they can be attached as notes to reports and office equipment, is a hundred million dollar innovation— developed simply because Frye found a need and filled it.

More and more, people are beginning to recognize creativity for what it really is. Today we realize that when a manager talks about creativity, he's not promoting the formation of an arts colony. He's discussing people and companies that have vision.

Innovation—Putting Creativity to Work for You

"Genius begins great works; labor alone finishes them."

French author Joseph Joubert (1754-1824) composed that succinct sentiment, and he might well have been talking about creativity versus innovation. Because, in today's results-oriented world, it's not enough just to have a vision—you must also be able to make that vison work. The innovator takes the clever, imaginative ideas of the creator and puts them to work. Without innovation, creativity is useless.

I once had an employee who was so creative that he lost all sight of the fact that to be useful, ideas have to be implemented. He'd come up with a fantastic, ingenious idea and everyone would busily set out to make it happen. Midway through that cycle, with everyone happily putting his idea into production, he'd come up with an even better way of doing it. So we'd all start over again. But before we finished on the improved plan, he'd come up with a super-improved version. The man was so creative he was never able to see anything through to conclusion. He was capable only of the creating, not the innovating.

Unlike the word *creativity*, the word *innovation* does not carry with it a load of preconceived notions. The world will allow an average businessman to be called innovative long before it will name him creative. And yet both abilities are vital if you want to tap into new energy in any organization.

Embracing Change Can Open the Door for Growth and Improvement

The major reason there are not more creative and innovative people in business is not that we are a nation of lazy, boring lunks. It's because creativity and innovation are scary. Why? Because they stand for change. And even though change often means growth and improvement, people resist it.

There are many reasons people resist the changes creativity brings, but the main one is this: change is difficult. Just as you get comfortable doing something one way, someone comes along and asks you to do it differently.

To get an idea of how hard it is to change, think about which side of the bed you sleep on. Is it always the same side? I definitely have "my side" of the bed, and my wife Shirley can't quite understand this. Sometimes I go to bed a little later than she does, and occasionally I come in and find her on *my* side. But when I nudge her and tell her that she's on my side she has the gall to ask, "What difference does it make?" Now that takes a lot of nerve! However, I want you to know I'm change oriented—as long as it doesn't involve me personally.

There are many other things people do by force of habit. Do you always take the same place at the dinner table? And when your in-laws come over and someone sits in *your* chair, do you get miffed? "Don't they know that's my chair?" you silently steam.

Everyone's negative reaction to change is quite normal. If you have very significant changes that accumulate, your stress levels go up and up. Pretty soon you look in the mirror and realize, "I've got wrinkles where I didn't used to wrinkle. And I sag and bag where I never did before." And when you notice these things, you think, "I don't like change. I really don't like change."

Change is threatening. And because creativity and innovation force change, they too become threatening. Some people don't want to be involved in creative ideas because of the demands the resultant changes will make on them. And others take every opportunity to put down creativity and those they think are creative—because, frankly, creative people make non-creative people look bad.

But even if the thought of dealing with change doesn't threaten you and you're not jealous of others who dream up brilliant ideas, implementing creativity means you have to *do* something. You'll have to take some type of action, and that can be annoying when you're comfortable in your routine.

Producing Tangible Results by Using Creativity and Innovation

If it's such an abrasive and strenuous process, why do people strive to be creative? What's the payoff?

People continue to create and innovate for one main reason: Creativity is a way of validating one's sense of worth. Just as God created, so we too want to create. When I visit New York or Philadelphia—the two graffiti capitals of the country, where everything that doesn't move gets painted—I'm amazed at the elaborate logos and symbols kids create. It's the same desire to be recognized and remembered that makes people carve on trees. They want to somehow say, "Kilroy was here."

Another big reason people strive to create is that creativity, when coupled with innovation, produces tangible results. Armed with these results, you'll have more options for attacking problems. All other things being equal, show me a person with options, and I'll show you a person who succeeds.

Allowing Yourself to Be Creative

After reviewing all the positive aspects of creativity and what it can do for you, I imagine you'd like to know how you can learn to be more creative. Contrary to popular belief, creativity is not a gift, it is a tool each of us possesses—if we just learn to use it.

For starters, learn to relax about the prospect of creating. Psychologist Rollo May, in his book *The Courage to Create*, (W.W. Norton and Company, 1975), talks about creativity occurring in the pauses of life. In other words, if you want to be creative, you've got to expose yourself to everything you can on a given topic, and then incubate it. Saturate yourself first, then remove yourself from it completely for awhile.

We've all done this successfully at one time or another. We'll turn an idea over to our subconscious and then wake in the middle of the night with a flash of brilliance. Or we may be driving, our mind meditating on the broken white line, when suddenly inspiration waves at us in the rear view mirror. Be prepared for such bursts of creative thinking by keeping a tape recorder or a pad and pencil around to record your thoughts.

Strengthening Your Creative Abilities Through Right Brain Development

Another method for increasing your imagination is to cultivate your right brain. In his excellent book *Take Effective Control of Your Life* (Harper & Row, 1984), William Glasser gives a great explanation of the right-brain/left-brain concept in creativity. In essence he explains it this way: There are right brain and left brain hemispheres. The left brain controls the right hand, and vice versa. The left brain is highly logical, and specializes in what we call linear/sequential thinking, recognizing patterns like, 1, 2, 3, 4, 5, and a, b, c, d, e, f, and so on.

Many teachers operate from the left brain. They say things like, "Okay, class, this semester we are going to cover 150 different areas, divided into 75 categories, and further divided into 42 subcategories." The left-brain students are thinking, "Oh boy, have we got this pegged." Meanwhile, the right-brain students, who are much more visually oriented, are sitting there looking at this teacher and thinking things like, "Gee, she sure looks like a giraffe."

If you learn to develop your right brain, you'll strengthen your creative abilities. One of the pluses of developing patterns of imagination is that they stay with you longer. Facts and numbers often slip our mind as quickly as we process them, but stories and pictures seem to stay with us forever. So, let the right brain invent the stories—and then the left brain can linear/sequentially examine these stories for possible implementation.

The Folly of Waiting for the Perfect Idea

One of the big holdbacks to people's being more creative is that everyone is waiting for another "sliced-bread idea" to come along. When you do get a good idea, what happens? You let the idea pass without ever discussing it with anyone or giving it a chance, because you're afraid it's not good enough and you wish you could think of a better one.

Have you sat in a meeting and come up with a good idea, and then thought, "Oh, everyone has probably already thought of that." You don't say anything and sure enough, someone else does come up with your idea, and she ends up with the credit.

Being a genius isn't really as hard as it looks. You've just got to learn to stick out your neck now and then.

Building an Organization That Innovates Can Propel You Toward Your Goals

Recently, I had the opportunity of participating in some extensive discussions on creativity with Jay Galbraith, Ph.D., a former faculty member at the Sloan School, MIT and Wharton. I spoke with Dr. Galbraith, who does management programs for companies such as Kodak, Procter & Gamble, and Fiat of Italy, about creating an organization that innovates.

One of Dr. Galbraith's initial comments about creativity was, "I've never met anyone who wouldn't rather be an entrepreneur than a bureaucrat. But every time we vote with our behavior rather than our words, bureaucracy always wins." In other words, innovativeness is something everyone is in favor of, but few ever achieve.

Just as individuals dread the change innovation brings, so do organizations—and with good reason. As Dr. Galbraith points out, "Innovation itself is a destructive process. It destroys investments that people have made. It destroys capital and careers." That's why everyone wants innovation, but they want it to affect someone else's investment. For example, the manufacturers of vacuum tubes were interested in innovation, but they were not happy to see semiconductors come along.

Another deterrent is the political nature of the process of innovation. Most organizations have been divided so that employees operate by charters and missions. Because new ideas violate those missions, innovators are constantly trespassing on other people's turf.

The third, and possibly the largest, obstacle to building an innovating organization is that innovation requires that the company be specifically designed for that purpose. Most companies, as Dr. Galbraith points out, are organized to do something for the millionth time, not for the first time. And any organization that is set up to do something well for the millionth time, is poorly organized to do something for the first time.

When you do something for the first time, you *want* to make mistakes. (Mistakes are a vital part of innovation, something I'll discuss later in this chapter.) It's critical that you find where the errors are and correct them. After the eighteenth or twentieth time, when you finally get it right, then you've developed the recipe or formula. On the other hand, on the operating side of an organization you don't want any surprises or uncertainty.

Companies that truly wish to be innovative need to have two modes of conducting activity—an operating mode and an innovating mode.

The idea behind separating the innovative and operational sides of a company is to provide a mechanism for trying out ideas on a small scale and keeping costs down. In fact, a separate budgeting process is a must. Once you've got your idea debugged and you've made your mistakes, you can roll it back into the rest of the organization, where it can really be leveraged.

But there is more to the innovating mode than just forming a "skunk works"—a separate operation in which to hatch ideas—or having breakthrough funds and special compensation awards. All of these need to be blended together in the innovative organization.

And although it's vital to have this division between operation and innovation, either physically or at least on paper, it's equally important not to put too much stress on the separation. If people are not free to move back and forth from one mode to the other, you create an elite group of "innovators," which shuts out others who may have inventive ideas of their own.

Structuring the Innovating Process

Teamwork is the key when it comes to setting up an innovating organization. Dr. Galbraith explains, "Innovation is not a single activity with one individual swimming upstream against the current." To ensure the success of new ideas, there are a number of roles that people in the company must play.

First is the role of the idea generator, the *champion* or entrepreneur who thinks of an idea and wants to run with it. Anybody in the organization can generate ideas; in fact, ideas typically come from the lower levels of an organization. So employees who have the most ideas are the least likely to do much about them. That's because they usually don't have the authority, credibility, or control over resources necessary to see their plans through.

That's where the second role, the *sponsor*, comes in. A sponsor is someone who can lend his credibility, authority, and access to resources to a project to get it going. Sponsors work to find funding for ideas that they think have a good chance of surviving. The other thing a good sponsor does is select ideas. But, he doesn't wait for ideas to come to him; he goes out and actively seeks them.

Dr. Galbraith tells of one manager who makes a habit of going into the company's research and development labs on Saturdays and Sundays. He looks for people who have come in to work on their own ideas—something they aren't supposed to do. If the manager likes an idea, he sponsors it. That means he works to find funding for it, encourages employees to get the data and results they need to prove the value of the idea, and then presents the idea and collateral material to the company leaders.

The third important role a company needs to fill is that of the *orchestrator*. This person, who is typically in upper management, is responsible for making sure that funding is allocated for the project and that the project fits in with the overall values of the organization. An orchestrator can play the role of sponsor at times. But her primary task is to direct the transitional process of moving

an idea from the unit where it was developed into the organizational mainstream—and making sure it flies once it's out of its
developmental cocoon. Without the overall coordination of an
orchestrator, most new ideas will flounder and eventually die.

Getting the funding to implement an idea is often the most
difficult obstacle on the road to innovation. In essence, the
company must provide what amounts to venture-capital funds.
And the best way to achieve this is to establish a separate
budget, as IBM does. According to Dr. Galbraith, in pursuing
independent business units, IBM makes available some $20
million per year. This money is specifically earmarked for
funding new business ideas which may previously have been
rejected in the normal business budgeting process.

As Dr. Galbraith is careful to point out, innovation is not
something that can be turned off and on. And when organizations don't separate out an innovating budget, one of the first
areas to suffer when money gets tight is the skunk works, or
"greenhouse," as it is sometimes called. To succeed at innovation, an organization must consistently support the people doing
the experimenting.

Another key element in the funding process is having
multiple sponsors. If the only sponsor an idea generator has
access to is his direct boss, and the boss doesn't like his idea,
that's usually the end of it. Everyone has certain blinders and
areas of disbelief. Outside the corporate world, an idea man
would take his invention or plan to banker after banker until he
found someone to back him. A company interested in fostering
creativity and inventiveness must try to simulate this same
procedure in-house.

Encouraging "Intracorporate Entrepreneurs" Fuels Growth

Once you have your skunk works set up in a separate area
with a separate budget and have made all the proper funding
arrangements, where do you find the people with the ideas? You

could go out and recruit creative, innovative people from other companies—but better still, why not develop them right there within your own organization?

From the employees and business leaders I've spoken with at seminars I've given across the country, I've learned that the most satisfied workers seem to be the ones who embody the entrepreneurial spirit—those whose companies encourage them to have vision. These employees know that there are no limits to what they can accomplish within their jobs and organizations. They don't feel pigeonholed, because they are given freedom to contribute to the company at all levels—not just within their immediate jobs or departments.

In 1978, management consultant Gifford Pinchot III, coined the term "intrapreneur," shorthand for "intracorporate entrepreneur." Pinchot, author of *Intrapreneuring: Why You Don't Have to Leave the Corporation to Become an Entrepreneur* (Harper & Row, 1985), defines the term "intrapreneur" as: "Any of the 'dreamers who do.' They are the people who take hands-on responsibility for creating innovation of any kind within an organization. The intrapreneur may be the creator or inventor, but he or she is always the dreamer who also figures out how to turn an idea into a profitable reality."

Freeing Employees to Experiment

To encourage intrapreneurship, it's essential that a company establish a secure environment in which dreamers are free to make mistakes. Failures and mistakes need not be embarrassing if you have created the right corporate culture. Employees should be made to realize that mistakes are an accepted and expected part of the growth process. Of course the objective is not to fail—but if you never take risks, you lose out on many opportunities. In fact, it's been said that when Thomas Edison experienced failure, he responded, "Results! Why, man, I have gotten a lot of results. I know several thousand things that won't work." And Italian economist Vilfredo Pareto has this to say about mistakes, "Give me a fruitful error anytime, full of seeds, bursting with its own corrections."

One company I know goes so far as to bestow a "No Guts, No Glory" award to the engineer who is chosen by his peers as the one who absolutely did the right thing, but it didn't work. To win this award you actually have to fail, but it has to be a good, worthwhile mistake from which others can learn.

Buckminster Fuller, of geodesic dome fame, is a great example of what can come from being allowed to make mistakes. At a program I attended with him in Mexico City, Fuller was asked to what he contributed his genius. He replied that he had never thought of himself as a genius. "I think I'm less inhibited than most people," he explained. My guess is that no one ever said to him, "That's a dumb idea, I can't believe you said that." I bet instead, when he said something, people responded by saying, "Ah, very interesting. Tell me more."

This type of uninhibited feeling is exactly what you want to encourage with the intrapreneurs you're trying to develop. Nothing kills creativity faster than inhibitions.

It is vital, then, to allow your creators and innovators to make mistakes; but it is equally important that you empower these people. Allow for risk, but at the same time help them realize that they have the ultimate responsibility for the task. Along with that accountability, be sure to give them authority, because one without the other is useless. If they don't have the authority to follow through with their projects, then all their creativity will be in vain.

If I have a high belief factor in the people with whom I work, then I have less anxiety. If an employee makes a mistake, he'll probably also come up with the answer to the mistake. In fact, he will probably work harder to come up with that answer since it was his mistake. And as a manager, the less I try to play God, the lower my anxiety and stress level will be.

Companies make the mistake of going part way toward creating this innovative environment, then nullifying everything by making a simple punitive move or response. A slap on the wrist over one or two items can undo all the positive things an employee has accomplished. It's somewhat like a salesperson who spends 20 minutes making the sale and the next 20 minutes buying the product back. You must be consistent in your support of innovativeness.

Another important element in the construction of a creative environment is the protection of new ideas. A new idea is very fragile. If you immediately start treating it as if it has the same status as a fully developed plan, you'll kill it. Don't jump all over it for some little practical concern. Allow it time to incubate and grow.

Motivating and Rewarding Invites Creative Solutions

What motivates people to be creative and innovative? Why do they take risks? How can you get someone to try something for the nineteenth time, when the first eighteen times didn't work? What drives these people?

There are as many answers to those questions as there are managers in this country. Some companies feel that monetary rewards, gifts, incentive travel programs, and special recognition awards are the best motivators. Other organizations would disagree strongly. Many managers would say you can create a great deal of motivation by providing people with the opportunity and the autonomy to do their own thing—a chance to see their fingerprints on something.

Promotion and recognition systems are used by some firms to reward people who have contributed creatively to the organization. Companies that believe peer recognition is an important part of motivation often bestow special awards and form distinguished societies for their innovators. Others find that the work itself is often the primary motivator.

But the one thing that each of the proponents of these different awards would probably agree on is this: motivation is the anticipation of achievement. And to keep a person motivated, there must be frequent anticipation of achievement.

Getting Serious About Play: Learn to Make Allowances for Humor

One aspect of encouraging an innovating organization, often overlooked by well-intentioned companies, is the importance of play. To encourage creativity and innovation, allowances must be made for humor and play. Play is the reward of an active mind. There is a hangover from the old puritan work ethic that work is serious business: if you're fooling around, you can't be producing. But in fact, the opposite may be true. A playful atmosphere often encourages the most creative of suggestions.

There are at least two important functions that play and humor can serve. First, play provides an uninhibited way of learning. Just watch a child at play. For children, their play is their work. They concentrate very hard on it, and in the process they learn things—at an incredible rate, too—about the world around them.

The other vital function that play serves, is release for tension and pressure. This is evident in the intensive-care units of most hospitals. When the nurses take a break, they joke and laugh. For ten minutes they are able to escape from the intensity and solemnity of the job they do for eight or more hours a day. Hospital visitors may initially react with horror to this light-hearted attitude, but in fact the nurses' behavior is therapeutic. If they didn't learn to release the tension that builds up, they might eventually crack.

Sparking Creativity: Fourteen Steps to Encourage Innovators and Creators

Earlier in this chapter we discussed the role of a sponsor in an innovating organization. An important function of any sponsor, which we just touched on previously, is to select ideas, as well as go out and find innovations. There is a certain skill required for this function, but it is one that can be developed.

For one thing, there is a great deal of *self-selection* that goes on with intrapreneurs. They tend to separate themselves from the crowd by the commitment they show to their ideas and plans. They are willing to invest enormous amounts of what Dr. Galbraith terms "sweat capital." In other words, they are willing to do whatever it takes to bring their idea to fruition.

Some companies have successfully brought people with this sort of commitment to the forefront by holding internal trade shows. Employees who have ideas they think are worthwhile are invited to set up booths, then management and other employees tour the show to examine the offerings.

Another way a good sponsor discovers ideas and idea generators is to visit different areas of the company and pick up bits of information from each. Pretty soon the pieces start falling into place—and the next thing you know a new concept is born.

Sponsors must, however, realize that one of the quickest ways to kill innovation is to take a full-blown idea from the generator and assign its implementation to someone who has not "bought into it." To thrive, ideas need the support of believers.

Idea blending is another effective way to generate innovations. Don't restrict your research and development to just manufacturing. Take an idea and brainstorm about its marketing, technology, and distribution. Then put it all together in terms of a product or business.

Idea blending can happen in several ways. Some companies form task forces to call on various customers and assess their needs. They then return to the plant to spin off ideas and chose the ones the group wants to pursue.

Field engineers are great sources of this type of information. They know the technology and the customer. They know the illnesses as well as the cures, and they are able to put them together in formulas to solve problems.

Grumman Corporation made this method into a science. Their engineers would meet every aircraft carrier as it docked. They would have their airplane design engineers go below deck and debrief the maintenance crew, who loved talking to them. And the engineers would get new ideas to incorporate into their next product. Giving design people direct access to the customer can be very valuable.

I once read a great excerpt by Woody Allen that could serve as the format for a good sponsor. Allen was worried about an advanced culture threatening us. Rather than being thousands of years advanced, as you might expect, these people were simply 15 minutes ahead of us. No Buck-Rogers-type weapons of annihilation here. What bothered Allen was that these people would always be first in line at the movies. And they'd never be late for an appointment. That sort of lead time is just the competitive edge every good sponsor needs. Innovation must be driven by the idea that we need to be just a little ahead of everyone else.

One fairly simple way to give people an advantage, and keep them excited and interested, is to let them move from one department to another. That way they see how other sections of the organization operate, and they are exposed to new people and different ideas.

In the seminars I give to businesses and organizations around the country, I like to hand out a list of skills that I think every good leader should develop. It seems to sum up some of the things we've discussed in this chapter.

A Leader Encourages Creativity and Innovation by...
1. Clearly and frequently articulating goals and visions.
2. Providing the security that encourages a pioneering spirit.
3. Demonstrating trust, regard and appreciation for each individual.
4. Providing the resources and environment the employee needs to do the best job possible.
5. Being flexible and tolerant, and able to live with ambiguity.
6. Being enthusiastic, excited, expectant; asking questions.
7. Listening.
8. Offering warmth, encouragement, support; running interference.
9. Expecting failures and setbacks; being persistent in the face of disappointment.

10. Laughing.

11. Looking for strengths; encouraging, stretching, and growing.

12. Giving specific praise—freely and often.

13. Becoming a mentor and role model.

14. Providing opportunities for "stretch" experiences for others.

Yes, but . . .

—"Yes, creativity may be fine for bigger, better capitalized companies, but all I care about is whether the gadget I'm producing works."

Unfortunately, by buying into those old stereotypes of creativity as some weird, artistic gift, you could be costing yourself and your company some money and some valuable employees. The great thing about creativity and innovation is that they are not limited to any socioeconomic group. They are not restricted to those with college degrees or worldly experience. They are not the rantings of wild-eyed artists. Anyone from any level of any company can come up with a winning idea.

The next step is to make sure that there is someone who will listen to that idea, and steer the creator in the direction of the people with the money and resources to make that idea happen. If that happens, everyone can be the richer for it, both financially and emotionally. But before any of this can happen, there has got to be a commitment to the idea of creativity and innovation and a desire to tap new sources of energy.

—Yes, I would like to be the type of person who constantly finds better ways to do things, but how can I expand my imagination?

Being conditioned to look for better ways to do things takes a special mind set. Murray Spangler was locked into a job as a department store janitor and suffered the added discomfort of wheezing and coughing caused by all the dust his broom stirred up. Many people would have quit, but Spangler set out to find a better way to clean floors.

"Why not eliminate the broom?" he thought, looking for a way to suck up the dust. His question led to a crude but workable vacuum cleaner which a friend in the leather business, H.W. Hoover, financed. Can you guess the end to this story?

When looking for a better way to do things, ask yourself, "What if?" Question the assumptions of what is currently being done. One creative way to get in touch with new ideas is to consider the worst possible ways to do the job, and then flip those ideas over and think of the best ways to approach the task. One of the exciting payoffs of finding a better way to do something is the confidence you gain in your ability and a greater feeling of satisfaction in your work.

CHAPTER 10

Converting Potential into Action: Match the Right Amount of Energy with the Desired Result

Recently, the president of a large manufacturing company invested in a new computer system for his organization. He wanted only the best for his staff, so he equipped every secretary and engineer with terminals that tied into a powerful mainframe. Within a week, the secretaries were complaining that the computers were completely wrong for them.

"I spent thousands of dollars on each of those terminals, only to discover that all our secretaries wanted were dedicated word processors that would have cost less than half the amount," the president groaned. "What overkill! What a waste!"

Providing the resources employees need to do their jobs doesn't necessarily mean giving them the most expensive equipment or enrolling them in every training program that comes along. It means making just the *right* investment in training, staffing, and equipment to optimize employees' potential and achieve desired results.

In Chapter 5, we discussed the importance of evaluating your Return on Time Investments. Similarly, wise managers also compute their Return on Investment (ROI) for the energy and resources a task will require before determining how much staff time and budget to allocate to it.

Getting a good ROI is much like what a tennis pro is after. He wants the time he invested in training to show up in aces when he's competing in a tournament. To do that, one of the most important skills a player can master is learning to hit the ball with the center of the racket. When he finds that "sweet spot" on his racket, as John Jerome discusses in *The Sweet Spot in Time* (Avon Books, 1982), the player can exert less effort yet still have the control and power to hit the ball with power and accuracy.

In much the same way, a champion manager learns to position his or her department or company in a way that will maximize everyone's efforts. Think about how finding the "sweet spot" in various situations can make your life easier. For example, if you have a good relationship with someone you're working with, the two of you will accomplish a lot with little effort. But if you have a poor relationship, you'll have to work harder to achieve the same results. Instead of finding your "sweet spot," the two of you have developed mental tennis elbow, and that leads to constant irritation and discomfort.

Capitalize on Employee Input to Multiply the Efforts of Your Work Force

One way to find that "sweet spot" is to realize that the people you work and live with play a significant part in your achievement of personal and business success and satisfaction. Many managers used to think that the worst thing that could happen to a business was to introduce a product or service and have customers or clients reject it. Now, one of the worst things that can happen in business is to lack the support of the people who work selling your product or service.

Managers at the Marriott Corporation are taught that the most important business relationship they can develop is not with their customers—it's with their employees. New managers spend a week or two in workshops learning how to coach and counsel employees. They are taught how to work *with* employees—not merely to direct them—because at Marriott, employees always have some degree of input.

"When you have the interaction of a lot of people, conflict is inevitable," says Brendan Keegan, Marriott's Vice President of Human Resource Planning and Development. "So the managers at Marriott are taught conflict management, not conflict *repression*. The belief that, when it comes to the company's success, the employee is what really counts, is the driving force behind our organization."

While labor unions talk about employees' rights, Marriott focuses on employees' *needs*. "We're not perfect, but we're on the right track," continues Keegan. "We've created an environment where employees feel good about themselves and the product they represent. They know they are part of a winning team in an organization where the boss takes a personal interest.

"We are blessed that Marriott is a family-run business, which has a way of personalizing the whole organization. No matter where they go, Bill and Dick Marriott talk about their father. They are very aware of the fact that one of the key values of our company is the family. Employees don't feel they're performing tasks for a nameless, faceless organization. They feel a part of something. They're not just carrying on tasks, they're carrying on the Marriott tradition of hospitality. That's the magic of Marriott."

When Marriott opens a hotel or other service, it flies in a team of experienced hourly employees, supervisors, and managers to the new site. "They stand alongside the new employees at that facility and teach them their jobs," explains Keegan. "Marriott is recruiting employees from the same labor pool as everyone else, so we're not necessarily picking the most hospitable or the most cordial people. We hire them and then really make them feel part of the whole Marriott experience."

Keegan says that when Marriott brings in managers from new acquisitions they are often quite shocked at how high the company sets its goals. For example, when a budget is established for a unit, the unit manager takes the budget not as a broad goal but as a very personal goal. "We have high goals and high degrees of personal commitment," says Keegan. "Marriott is a winner; we don't like to lose."

Optimizing Effectiveness: Learn to Redistribute Your Energy and That of Your Employees

Optimizing effectiveness requires that we use our energy in the most precise way. That means taking an honest look at how we spend our time. There may be areas you should be paying attention to but you can't because you're spending attention on things that don't deserve it. Ask yourself: Is it really necessary to attend all those committee meetings? Am I performing half of my assistant's job instead of expecting him to bear his own weight? Do I resurrect dead issues and beat them to death even though I should have learned my lesson from them months ago?

Next, let yourself challenge policies and procedures. What amenities would optimize workers' productivity in the work station? Can employees take the portable computer terminal home over the weekend to meet an upcoming deadline? What other ways can you redistribute your and your employees' energies?

You can also apply the principal of matching the appropriate amount of energy with the desired result in your personal life. It's your choice. You can go home at the end of the day feeling and looking like a wrung-out dishrag, or you can pace yourself and have energy left over for yourself and your family.

To me, optimizing performance doesn't mean doing something as well as someone else; it means doing as well as *you* possibly can in a given situation. The end result of optimizing our performance should be personal satisfaction, not one-upmanship.

If I had tried to "keep up with the Joneses" when I was growing up, I would have lost every time I tried. When I was a teenager and wanted a car, the only one I could afford was in pretty bad shape. It was badly dented on the outside, and the seats and floor mats were falling apart. But I was determined to make it the best it could be. I waxed it—I even waxed over the rust spots—and vacuumed it. It still didn't look great, but it looked better than it had. When it needed mechanical repairs, I'd buy parts from other cars in the junk yard and make the car run. That car represented my ability to convert potential into action.

Norman Cousins told me that he believes human beings are born with the ability to respond to challenge. That's why so many people diagnosed with terminal illnesses are able to live a lot longer than predicted. They don't deny their illness, but they do deny the verdict that goes with it. And it's those people who, no matter what their circumstances, get more out of life than others.

Even though he still keeps a hectic schedule, Cousins says he has more fun now than he did before his illness. "On my way back from lunch today, I sat in the quadrangle outside the cafeteria and watched the parade of people go by," he said when I visited him in his office at UCLA. "I don't think that is something I would have done a few years ago. I also program a weekly golf game into my schedule."

Cousins has managed many hundreds of people during his career, but he stresses that he never drove them. "I tried to be a cheerleader. To make them feel that what they were trying to do was possible. And when they confronted obstacles, I tried to help them overcome them."

The message Cousins left with me is that he doesn't believe in setting limitations; and he never quits before he tries. That's a wise and valid philosophy. I've allowed self-doubt or narrow-minded thinking to limit me at times. Now, when I start to fall prey to self-defeating behavior, I remind myself that I own my own life and that I have great capacities. And I tell myself that I have a lot of control over what happens to me, and *complete* control over how I respond to what happens to me. That way I am the victor, not the victim.

Consistency: The Secret to Professionalism

The secret to professionalism is to be able to do your best time after time, in a variety of situations. A professional is someone who will complete what needs to be done even if he doesn't feel like doing it. An amateur is somebody who can't do what needs to be done—even when he feels like it.

A lot of people perform well on a periodic basis, but consistency is what makes a pro. Given enough chances, I might do as well as any golf pro on one hole of golf. But that might be the only time I do it, whereas Tom Watson hits that well almost every time he plays. The symphony conductor Leonard Bernstein doesn't just give one great concert a year; every time he gets out there he's a winner.

The secret to success is being able to hit the sweet spot consistently and knowing how to adjust your approach if you begin to falter. At work, you may not be able to hit the sweet spot with all your employees every day. But because you're a pro, you know that if you hit too high or too low, you have the skills, expertise, and discipline to know how to adjust your swing the next time. You don't solve problems merely by trying harder and exerting more energy. You need to practice carefully, pay acute attention, and have the wherewithal to position yourself where you'll get the most power.

One of the secrets to being able to work well on a consistent basis is to learn how to get the best advantage out of our energy. As I discussed earlier, that means we have to manage our resources by asking, "Is this the best possible use of our time, energy, and resources?" Flexible work schedules came about when management realized that employees had different times of peak performance. Some people work best in the quietness of morning. Others are just getting revved up after lunch and can power out until late into the evening.

Stew Leonard of Stew Leonard Dairy knows exactly what schedule he needs to keep to do his best consistently. Each morning at 5:30 a.m., he swims 40 laps in his pool and then stretches out in the spa for half an hour. He keeps a legal pad nearby to jot down ideas, notes, and things to do. By 7:30 a.m., he calls the dairy and his workday begins. By getting an early start on the day, Leonard is able to get the best return from the time and energy he invests.

Overcoming Obstacles: Refuse to Accept Negative Messages from Yourself or Others

I was on a program with and had the pleasure of hearing Vice-Admiral James Stockdale speak. He was shot down on a combat mission in Vietnam in 1965 and wasn't released until 1973. He spent much of his almost eight years of imprisonment in solitary confinement, where he said he discovered firsthand the capabilities and limitations of the human spirit.

Stockdale said his only weapons in prison were the very fiber and sinew of his soul. A structured set of values, supporting a basic tenet of self-respect, was fundamental to his surviving the prison ordeal—with all its degradation, misery, and pain. He did 400 push-ups a day, because as he said, self-discipline and ritual are vital to self-respect.

Stockdale wrote:

> In that brutally controlled environment a perceptive enemy can get his hooks into the slightest chink in a man's ethical armor and accelerate his downfall. Given the right opening, the right moral weakness, a certain susceptibility on the part of the prisoner, a clever extortionist can drive his victim into a downhill slide that will ruin his image, self-respect and life in a very short time.
>
> I am thinking of the tragedy that can befall a person who has such a need for love or attention that he will sell his soul for it.

Stockdale's captors were trying to force him to relinquish his personal integrity. But they were unsuccessful because he clung tightly to his sense of self-esteem. He concluded early on that he was not a victim, but captain of his own soul. Stockdale goes on to explain how he accomplished this:

> To keep integrity, your dignity, your soul, you have to retain responsibility for your actions, to deal with guilt... You need to look squarely at what you did and measure its limited gravity in the light of the overall truth of the total situation, then use the guilt, such as it is, as a cleansing fire to purge the fault, as a goad for future resolve, and above all not be consumed by it.

The enemy couldn't make Stockdale cave in because he wouldn't accept negative messages of worthlessness from his captors—or from himself. Sometimes we let past events in our life hold us captive. We feel guilty about having done something and continually castigate ourselves for it, rather than learning from the mistake and moving on. There is a big difference between feeling remorse for what we've done and feeling guilty about it. When we are remorseful, we regret what's happened, apologize if necessary, and learn from the experience. Guilt, on the other hand, is something that gnaws away at us, making us feel as if we're terrible, inadequate people.

Instead of dwelling on mistakes, optimal performers overcome obstacles and transcend previous accomplishments. They are challenged to do things better than what they've done before. Don't be concerned with what others do to you—it's what you do to you that is important. Just think how wonderful it would be if you could stretch your mind much further than it has been stretched before. Or how great it would be to love someone even more than you did before—or to have their love for you transcend previous bounds. It's certainly something worth considering!

Fulfill Your Potential by Discovering What Life Is Expecting from You

I believe that two needs that are essential to all lives are meaning and purpose. My first introduction to that notion came from reading *Man's Search for Meaning: An Introduction to Logotherapy* (Simon & Schuster, 1959), by psychiatrist Viktor Frankl, a survivor of the concentration camps of Auschwitz and Dachau. Frankl said that in many cases, the people who survived the death camps were not those who were the strongest physically but the ones who kept meaning and purpose in their lives.

Prisoners in the death camp were given a bowl of broth and two cigarettes a day. Frankl said he frequently saw prisoners who had lost their will exchange their broth for cigarettes. In other words, they were giving up nourishment for cigarettes because they had lost all reason for living.

Frankl developed what is referred to as "Logotherapy" or "Meaning Therapy" out of repeated proof that those who find special meaning in life, even in a death camp, are the ones who will have a better chance to endure adversity.

He reported on two would-be suicide cases, involving two men who bore striking similarities to one another. Both men were about to commit suicide because they believed they had nothing more to expect from life. According to Frankl, the men had to realize that life still expected something from them.

For one man, the something to live for was his child whom he adores; for the other, a scientist, it was a series of books he had started writing and still had to finish. This man's work could not be completed by anyone else, and no one could be the biological father of the other man's child.

Frankl says in his book, "When the impossibility of replacing a person is realized, it allows the responsibility which a man has for his existence and its continuance to appear in all its magnitude. A man who becomes conscious of the responsibility he bears toward a human being who affectionately waits for him, or an unfinished work, will never be able to throw away his life."

The secret of life seems to lie in the belief that life is still expecting something from us. And if we couple that with expecting the best from ourselves—both personally and professionally—we can't help finding the "sweet spot" time after time.

How to Escape Your Comfort Zones and Achieve More

Optimal performers avoid comfort zones—those little pockets of existence where we do just enough to get by without exerting ourselves. Can you say that about your life? Do you avoid comfort zones or are you tucked in tight for the winter? I believe that being too comfortable is dangerous. In fact, that's one of the problems we have in the United States—we've got a pretty heavy comfort zone. Just look at voter turnouts. Many people vote *if* it's convenient; that's a big comfort zone.

The same thing happens in business. Success makes us fat and sassy. "Who can touch us?" we ask. But isn't it interesting that the majority of companies that dominated our economy at the turn of the century no longer exist today?

And we get a bit too comfortable in our personal lives, too. We don't know what's wrong with our marriage, but it sure isn't worth the effort needed to make it better. We'd be much better off if we lived by the following Marshall McLuhan expansion on a Buckminster Fuller philosophy: On the spaceship earth there are no passengers; we're all crew. In other words, I hold up my end and you hold up yours.

We'd be eager to hold up our end if we had goals within us that burned with conviction. As Friedrich Nietzsche wrote "He who knows a *why* for living, will surmount almost every *how*." Having goals can give you hope, and hope translates into action.

Just think if we had a whole office full of people who took responsibility for what needed to be done. Imagine an entire household of optimal performers. It's fun to work and live with people like that because, instead of wasting time complaining, they spend time getting things done.

Running in Your Target Zone Will Keep You at the Front of the Pack

Several years ago, I bought a device to measure my heartbeat while I run. I'd been running for 20 years and was happy with my ability to run in a 10K and pass people half my age. I'd think, "Fred, you're doing all right."

I decided to use the monitor to make sure I was getting the most out of running. The unit works this way: You set your target heart rate on the monitor. If you don't reach the target zone, the unit beeps. When you get to the target zone it falls silent. If you go over target rate, it beeps rapidly. In other words, working your heart too much is as bad or worse than working it too little.

The first day I strapped on the unit, I began running at my normal pace and it started to beep. I thought "Surely my heart is working harder than that." I picked up the pace. No change. It wasn't until I was running much faster that I entered my target zone, and the darn unit shut up.

I thought I was working pretty hard, but the *unit* said, "Pryor, you're dogging it. You're loafing compared to what you could be doing. And you're not getting the value that you could be getting."

Since that experience, I've often thought it would be neat to have a device like that to monitor other areas of our lives. When we are trying to slide by and not giving something our all, it would beep, "Nope, you're not even coming close to your potential." And when we are working too hard and ignoring our families, it would warn us, "Hey, you're doing too much of this."

A lot of us do work too much. We over-obligate ourselves because we keep saying, "Yes, yes, yes." And saying yes to too many things is the same as saying "No" to something else. Think for a minute. How many times have you said "Yes" to a client and had to work a weekend? Isn't that the same thing as saying "No" to your family or other areas that need balance? And have you really wanted to do something, but with all your obligations and commitments you just couldn't find the time?

Remember, running too hard can be just as dangerous as not running hard enough. And if there are areas of your life where you're coasting, you're not stretching and thus not getting the most from yourself. Ask yourself what will happen if you continue to live with the same frustrations that have been pulling you down for months—even years? Chances are, if you invested the same energy in positive areas instead of burning it up with anxiety, you'd live a much more satisfying life.

When you're running in your target zone, the effort you expend becomes an investment. Larger-than-life people often look as if they are blessed with more energy and intelligence than the average Joe or Josephine, but they're not. They have simply learned to channel their energies in ways that work to their betterment, not to their detriment. And they set no limits on what is possible for themselves.

Tacking into the Wind: Using Available Resources to Achieve Your Objectives

It doesn't take much skill or character to be an optimal performer when something good is happening to you. The real test is when things seem to be working against you.

Consider the concept of "tacking into the wind." This is a sailing term for the delicate process of using a wind coming out of the north to travel north or a wind coming out of the south to travel south. By putting the bow at angles to the wind, and skillfully using both the rudder and sail, you can make a wind that is blowing one way propel you in the opposite direction.

Those who know about "tacking" know that it is possible to use whatever forces there are to achieve your objectives. They are the ultimate optimists. They don't use their energies in destructive ways. But they continually remind themselves of the possibilities.

When adversity or challenge comes along, start "tacking into the wind." Use your skills and knowledge to face the forces and make them work for you. Keep looking for the possible. Be creative and let your mind explore alternative solutions. Develop confidence in yourself by accepting challenges and proving yourself continually. Finally, remember that the lessons we gather from experience are called wisdom.

Maintaining the Energy Cycle: Overcoming Fatigue and Renewing Excitement

Finding, maintaining, and optimizing your energy and that of your employees is essential to business success. But don't think that you can be a peak performer 24 hours a day, 365 days a year. Give yourself permission to cycle—to have big bursts of energy and occasional slumps. When you are in a slump, the first thing to do is to recognize it, but don't beat yourself over the head for it. Remind yourself that it's a natural part of the process.

You may even want to plan for "downtimes" by saving projects that don't demand a lot of concentration and creativity for times when your fuel supply is on reserve. In reality, people do this all the time. You know that if you've been doing mental tasks all day, you may be too tired to go home and read, but not too tired to work out at the gym and get physical. And a mother who has been with the kids all day feels depleted of energy for her kids, but knows she'll become rejuvenated if she can just spend some time alone or with adults.

Energy also plays musical chairs within the five energy hot spots of your organization. You may have focused for months on employee morale and feel tapped out in that area, but find new energy if you begin concentrating on marketing your product. Or perhaps all the energy directed to human resources can be spread out among two or three other areas to give them each a little boost.

If ways of cycling energy don't occur naturally in your organization, orchestrate them. Maslow found in his studies that people who have more evolved or highly developed personalities have more peak experiences than those who limit themselves (*Toward a Psychology of Being*, 1968). I like to have several things going at once so that while one project is cooking, another is just popping out of the oven, and I'm gathering ingredients for still another.

Probably the best way to keep our energy cycle going as strong as possible is to celebrate accomplishments. Remember, what gets rewarded, gets done. If you allow your child to throw a tantrum to get what he wants, he simply continues to practice that skill and you get lots of first-class tantrums. If you don't give him what he wants when he misbehaves, he quickly gets the message that his behavior won't get him anywhere. The same holds true with employees. If you reward lethargic behavior and late reports, you will continue to get exactly that.

Every management task you perform is not just creating products and services, it's creating people. And when employees feel that their manager really wants to build them up and make them strong, he begins behaving that way.

If you want to be an energetic leader, become the director of your life and provide others with the resources they need to meet their goals. As life moves, you need to move with it and learn to change. That's not bad news; it's good news. Change excites and energizes us and puts us in control. I'd like to challenge you to commit to making choices that will not only empower *you*, but those around you as well. It may not be the way everyone else manages, but it will guarantee you the most satisfaction and success.

INDEX

A

Achievement Loop, 85-86
Actions, as reflection of values, 84-89
Adelizzi, Robert, 35-38, 40
Allen, Woody, 169
Anger, 68
Ascent of Man, The,
Autocratic management, 102-3

B

Bernstein, Leonard, 178
Bethy's Bakery, 137
Bottom-up management, 102-4
Bronowski, Jacob, 20
"Brownouts," communication, 120-21
Buck-passing, 20-21
Buscaglia, Leo, 129

C

Celebration, 74, 76-77
Change
  adapting to , 35-39
  bias against, 113-14
  corporate mission statement for, 40-41
  creativity and, 157
  fear of, 33-35, 38-39, 157
  goals and momentum of, 64-67
  management of, 39-40
  monitoring of, 41-43
Change Masters, The, 10-11
Clance, Pauline Rose, 33
Coleman, George, 52-53
Comfort zones, 181-82

Commitment, leadership style and, 110-11
Communication, lines of, 115-31
  allowing for mistakes, 118
  "brownouts," 120-21
  confidential information and, 127-29
  effective versus ineffective approaches, 124
  extra-verbal, 122-23, 126-27
  feedback, 116-18, 125-26, 131, 135
  gripes, 120-21, 123-26
  hidden messages, 123
  listening, 78, 129-31
  mirroring techniques and, 127
  nonverbal, 126-27
  resourcing manager versus controlling manager and, 124-25
  rumors, 121-22
  speaking employees' language, 119
Confidential information, 127-29
Consistency, professionalism and, 177-78
Controlling manager
  communication approach of, 124-25
  resourcing manager versus, 106, 108-9, 124-25
Conwell, Russell Herman, 45-46
Corporation as a product of trust, 99-114
Courage to Create, The, 158
Cousins, Norman, 62, 177
Creativity
  allowing, 158-59
  change and, 157
  encouragement of "intrapreneurship", 163-66
  how to tap, 153-71

187

Creativity *(cont'd.)*
   innovation as a part of, 156
   motivation and, 166
   myth of, 154-55
   right brain development and, 159
   steps to encourage, 167-70
   tangible results from, 158
   waiting for the perfect idea, 159-60
Cunningham, Ed, 154, 155

D

Decision-making, play breaks and,
   147-48
Delegation, 73, 74-75, 95-96
   abuse of, 106-7
Dependency, avoiding employee, 105-7
Development and training, 142-44
Diffusion of Innovations, 38
Director, role of, 71-79
DIRECTORS system, 73-79
Disney, Walt, 136
Donnelly Corporation, 128-29

E

Edison, Thomas, 164
Effort, extra, 29-30
Empowerment, 74, 76
Energy Factor, definition of, 3-4
Energy robbers, 59-79
Excellence, commitment to, 28
Excitement
   how to build, 1-21
   how to renew, 184,86
Expectations, 112
External markets, 11-13
Extra-verbal communication, 122-23,
   126-27

F

Fatigue, overcoming, 184-86
Fear
   of change, 33-35, 38-39, 157
   conquering, 68
Feedback, 131, 135
   openness to, 116-18
   vague and general, 125-26

Fitness and health program, 145-47
Flexibility, importance of, 33-40
Focusing energy, 81-97
Frankl, Viktor, 180-81
Fry, Art, 33, 155
Fuller, Buckminster, 165, 182
Future
   how to move into the, 16-18
   the leader as visionary, 30-33
   long-range planning, 23-43
   present as basis for the, 48-49, 149-50

G

Galbraith, Jay, 160, 161, 162, 163, 168
Game plan, 5-6
Game playing, how to develop teamwork
   from, 63-64
Glasser, William, 34, 159
Goals
   company, 5-8
   goal-orientation, 113
   innovation and, 160-61
   momentum of change and, 64-67
Gore, Wilbert, 19-20, 134-35, 141, 150
W.L. Gore & Associates, Inc., 19-20,
   134-35, 141
Gore-Tex, 19
Gripes, 120-21, 123-26
Grumman Corporation, 168-69

H

Hallmark Cards, Inc., 117, 118, 154, 155
Health and fitness program, 145-47
Heiple, Rhonda, 53
Hewlett-Packard, 151
Hidden messages, 123
Hiring new employees
   synergy and, 140-42
   using intuition in, 141-42
Hojel, Richard, 66-67
Home Federal Savings and Loan, 35-38,
   40, 41
Hookless Fastener Company, 113-14
Hoover, H.W., 171
Hospital Corporation of America, 40-41
Hot spots of organizational energy
   description of, 8-15

how to activate potential energy
within, 15-16
Human resources, 9-10
Humor, 167

I

IBM, 163
Imposter Phenomenon, 33
*Imposter Phenomenon, The: Overcoming
the Fear That Haunts Your Success*,
33
In and Out the Garbage Pail, 120-21
Inertia, how to conquer, 1-21
Information systems, 13-15
Inner custodian, 73, 75
Innovation
champion of, 162
encouragement of "intrapreneurship",
163-66
goals and, 160-61
mistakes and, 161, 164-65
orchestrator of, 162-63
as a part of creativity, 156
play and, 167
sponsor of, 162, 163
steps to encourage, 167-70
structuring of, 162-63
teamwork and, 162-63
In Search of Excellence, 77
Intensity, leadership style and, 110-11
Interest, 113
Interruptions, 93-94
Interviewing a potential employee, 79
*Intrapreneuring: Why You Don't Have to
Leave the Corporation to Become
an Entrepreneur*, 164
"Intrapreneurship", 163-66
Intuition, hiring new employees and,
141-42
Investing in employees, 104-5

J

Jacques, Elliot, 30-31
Jerome, John, 174
Joubert, Joseph, 156
Journal, keeping a personal, 41-42

K

Kanter, Rosabeth Moss, 10-11
Keegan, Brendan, 175-76
Knister, Jim, 128-29
Know-how, 112
Kroc, Ray, 149
Kuhn, Thomas S., 34-35

L

Law of the Slight Edge, The, 30
Leader(s)
earning the right to be a, 150
how to develop a company of, 18-21
how style influences commitmeent
and intensity, 110-11
team spirit and, 50-55
ultimate responsibility of a, 18
as visionary, 30-33
Learners, types of, 129-30
Leonard, Beth, 137
Leonard, Stew, 136-38, 178
List, To Do, 89-90
Listening, 78, 130-31
types of, 129-30
*Listening with the Third Ear: The Inner
Experience of a Psychoanalyst*, 78
Loehr, Brad, 56-57
Long-range planning, 23-43
Love, Phil, 82, 119
Lyons, Fred W., Jr., 39

M

McClelland, June, 52
McDonald's, 149
McLuhan, Marshall, 182
Management styles
autocratic, 102-3
bottom-up, 102-4
controlling, 106, 108-9, 124-25
resourcing, 106, 108-9, 124-25
*Man's Search for Meaning: An
Introduction to Logotherapy*, 180-81
Marconi, Marchese Guglielmo, 113
Marion Laboratories, Inc., 11, 19, 38-40,
87-88
Marriott, Bill, 119, 175

Marriott, Dick, 175
Marriott Corporation, 117-18, 174-76
Maslow, Abraham, 107, 185
Matching energy with result, 173-86
May, Rollo, 158
Meaning in life, importance of, 180-81
Mirroring techniques, 127
Mission statement, corporate, 40-41
Mistakes
    allowing for, 118, 161, 164-65
    communication and, 118
    innovation and, 161
Monitoring of change, 41-43
Motivation, 7-8
    creativity and, 166
    recognition as part of, 53-54, 166
Murray, Mike, 126
Mushroom Principle, 13

N

National Aeronautics and Space
    Administration (NASA), 145
Needs, meeting employees', 67-68
Negativism, 179-80
Nemergut, Stephen, 51-52, 53
Nietzsche, Friedrich, 182
Nonverbal communication, 126-27
Nuclear Fuels Division, Westinghouse,
    6-8, 88

O

Obstacles, overcoming, 179-80
Optimism, 74, 77-78
Optimization of effectiveness, 176-77
Organizational structure, 10-11
Organizing, efficient, 91-92, 97
Ownership, 113

P

Pareto, Vilfredo, 29, 91, 164-65
Pareto's Law, 91
Participation, 111-12
PERKS system, 111-12
Perls, Frederick S., 120-21
Peter Principle, 96
Pinchot, Gifford III, 164
Planning, long-range, 23-43

Play
    decision-making and, 147-48
    innovation and, 167
    learning to, 144-45
Post-it® Note, 155
Potential, development of full, 45-58,
    180-81
Power Tower, 153-54
Present, as basis for the future, 48-49,
    149-50
Prima donna, role of, 70-71, 133
Priorities, 89-90, 97
Productivity, how to cultivate, 2-4
Professionalism
    consistency and, 177-78
    definition of, 177-78
Pryor Resources, Inc., 16-18, 81-82, 115,
    116, 119, 135, 142
Purpose in life, importance of, 180-81
Pygmalion, 65

R

Radically present, 74, 78
Recognition, 111, 112
    as part of motivation, 53-54, 166
Redistribution of energy, 176-77
Reik, Theodore, 78
Reiterate, Remind, Review, and
    Remember, 54-55
Resourcing manager
    communication approach of, 124-25
    controlling manager versus, 106,
        108-9, 124-25
Responsibility, 113
Rest and relaxation, importance of, 145
Result, matching energy with, 173-86
Return on Investment (ROI), 174
Return on Time Investments (ROTI),
    90-91
Risk, 74, 75-76
Rockefeller, John D., 109
Rogers, Everett M., 38
Roosevelt, Eleanor, 63
Rumors, 121-22

S

Satisfaction, 112

Scheduling, 92-93
Schweitzer, Albert, 28, 29
Self-esteem, support network and, 107-8
Self-Obstructing Behavior (SOB), 60-63
Simplot, J.R., 149-50
Sisyphus, 29
Slember, Dick, 6-8, 88
Socrates, 29
Spacek, Sissy, 33
Spangler, Murray, 170-71
Specialized Systems, Inc. (SSI), 50-53, 56-57
Spirit, team, 50-55
Stew Leonard's Dairy Store, 136-38, 178
Stockdale, James, 27, 179-80
Strengths
   helping employees size up their, 55-58
   questions for assessing a company's weaknesses and, 49-50
Structure of Scientific Revolutions, 34-35
Support from employees, importance of, 174-76
Support network, self-esteem and, 107-8
Sweet Spot in Time, The, 174
Synergy
   hiring new employees and, 140-42
   steps to increase, 138-40

T

Tacking into the wind, concept of, 184
Take Effective Control of Your Life, 34, 159
Talon Manufacturing, 114
Tandem Computers, Inc., 14, 54, 151
Target zone, 182-83
Task force, example of an everyday, 134-36
Team spirit, 50-55
Teamwork
   how to change game playing into, 63-64
   how to cultivate, 2-4
   innovation and, 162-63
   maximizing energy through, 133-51

Technology, 13
Teleconferencing, 88
Telephone calls, 94-95
Testing, 74, 77
This Is My Story, 63
3M, 33, 155
"Tough Love," 21
Toward a Psychology of Being, 107 185
Toynbee, Arnold, 34-35
Training and development, 142-44
Treybig, James, 14-15, 151
Truman, Harry, 97
Trust, cooperation as a result of, 99-114
Tunnel vision, 4-5

U

Understudy, role of, 69-70
University of Kansas, 17

V

Values, actions as reflection of, 84-49
VIGOR system, 112-13
Visionary, the leader as, 30-33
Vitality, 113

W

Watson, Tom, 178
Weaknesses, questions for assessing a company's strengths and, 49-50
Westinghouse, Nuclear Fuels Division of, 6-8, 88
Wheeler, Larry, 38-40, 87-88
Worrying, 69

Y

Yamaha, 41
Young Presidents Organization, Inc. (YPO), 66, 149, 150